†

William Biersach's character of Fr. John Baptist is a rare commodity: he's a real man's man; the kind who used to flock to the priesthood because the greatest opponent a man could face was supreme evil, the greatest battle to be won was the salvation of souls.

—Bill Means—
St. Louis, Missouri

†

Professor Biersach's Father Baptist mysteries are proof that supernatural evil still needs to be exorcized in traditional fashion. It can't continue to be swept under the chair (or cathedral). *The Search for Saint Valeria,* the third in the series, promises to take us deeper beneath the darkened conscience of the postconciliar American Church. As Father Baptist and Martin Feeney confront the darkness, Biersach makes us shudder in horror and laugh out loud in recognition. And there are a lot of good laughs to be had.

—Margaret Robe Summit, Ph. D—
Everett, Washington

†

I read literally all night, my heart pounding with anticipation, fear or excitement, turning pages almost faster than I could read. I read all the next day, and into the night as well, having cooked *no* meals for the family, ignored the laundry, the telephone, the computer ... and everything else! Before purchasing *The Endless Knot* or *The Darkness Did Not,* do take the time to at least buy TV dinners and arrange for a babysitter! Then—guilt free—inhale some of the best mystery stories ever written!"

—Constance Korte—
Wichita, Kansas

†

If you never thought you could howl with laughter while sheer terror stands your hair on end—read this book!

—Lucy Cook—
Brunswick, Ohio

†

The Darkness Did Not: It's better than broccoli!

—Mark Alessio—
Point Lookout, NY

†

Sherlock Holmes and Dr. Watson, Hercule Poirot and Hastings—move over! Fr. John Baptist and his chronicler, Martin Feeney, are every bit as endearing as their better-known counterparts. The characters are well-drawn. You'll come to think of them as friends. The plots are fascinating, the events cathartic, *and* you've given an inside view of the world of radical traditional (rad/trad) Catholicism. I simply couldn't put them down until I had read each one twice!

—Annette F. Wilcox, MA—
Moshi, Tanzania

†

I just love Mr. Biersach's books.
They combine all my favorite things:
the Catholic faith, murder mystery, and laughter.
As a matter of fact I have laughed so hard
in some places it brought tears to my eyes.
I will admit I have even underlined parts I didn't want to forget.

—Pamela Klemenz—
West Haven, Connecticut

†

William Biersach gives a whole new meaning
to working out one's salvation in fear and trembling.

—Marianna Bartold—
Lapeer, Michigan

P.S. Comment from my 17 year old daughter, Bernadette:
"Don't read TDDN at night!"
And from our 14 year old son, Stephan,
budding writer and aspirant to the Knights Tumblar:
"Mr. Biersach has written books of light and truth,
and the darkness will not comprehend it."

†

Not just for Catholics. William Biersach's mystery novels will crowd right to the top of anyone's "Favorites" list! A tip: Don't pass these books around. You'll *never* get them back!

—Anne Hale—
Grants Pass, Oregon

†

Biersach creates a unique mystery plot,
incorporates long-forgotten spiritual forces,
fine tunes his character development,
humorously exploits the Novus Ordo antics of the modern Church,
while he simultaneously remains theologically correct.
Pure genius!

—Ænola Koob—
Minneapolis, Minnesota

†

Just when we thought we had it, there was another twist.
The characters are so real that we think we know them.
With about thirty books on the shelf to be read right now,
I could not put *The Endless Knot* down!
Still checking it because more details come to light with each reading.
Underlined the first novel ever.
MORE! MORE! I'm beggin' for MORE, ya hear?

—Kathy Hicks—
Olney, Maryland

†

What a wonderful group of characters! Biersach brings each of them to life in uncanny detail. You'll find yourself wanting to drive down to St. Philomena's to watch it all in person. It's hard to shake the belief that they're really there. A word of caution: you'll want to stock up on plenty of freezer dinners and make sure the laundry's done before you open this book because the rest of the family will have to fend for themselves until the last page is read. I can't remember the last time I've enjoyed a book this much.

—Dena Suarez—
Lake Katrine, New York

The Search for Saint Valeria

The Search for Saint Valeria

by

William L. Biersach

TUMBLAR HOUSE
Bona Tempora Volvant

Arcadia
MMV

Nihil Obstat: *Huh?*

✣   Imprimatur: *Are you kidding!?!?*

ISBN: 0-9712786-2-8

First printing: 2005

Manufactured in the U.S.A.
by
Tumblar House
PMB 376
411 E. Huntington Drive, #107
Arcadia, CA 91006
www.tumblarhouse.com

The Search for Saint Valeria

*The third book in the continuing saga of
Fr. John Baptist, the cop-turned-priest, and
Martin Feeney, his gardener-turned-chronicler.*

This book is gratefully dedicated to

Julia Ulano

Faithful Friend and proofreader extraordinaire
Who stood fast during the bleakest of times.

How shall we sing the song of the Lord
in a strange land?
If I forget thee, O Jerusalem,
let my right hand be forgotten.

—Psalm CXXXVI: 4-5

Other books by

William L. Biersach

∞

Published by Tumblar House

The Endless Knot
The Darkness Did Not

Published by Catholic Treasures

Of Mary There Is Never Enough

0

AUTHOR'S NOTE (written seven years before publication): "I will concede," I said to myself as I sat down on the Feast of St. John Chrysostom to begin writing this story, "that Martin Feeney and I do have some things in common." A couple of companions, you see—the kind of friends who don't begrudge reading the manuscripts of their as yet unpublished associates, God bless 'em!—had confided to me over drinks the night before that they had pictured *me* in the role of Martin as they read his memoirs. "Martin and I happen to share the same birthday," I continued musing to myself, "the Feast of St. Philip Neri, the 'Laughing Saint,' which explains the similarities in our senses of humor. I do have a back problem, but it isn't the same as his. My spiritual life has similarly been defined by my struggle to keep and practice my Faith amidst the havoc and desecration left behind by the V2 bomb; and as I embark on my third tale in the series, its prequels remain unpublished. Beyond that, I don't think so. Besides, Martin is quicker on his feet with comebacks, not to mention far more familiar with Sacred Scripture than I could ever be—hence the Douay concordance on my coffee table. But, well, who knows?"

It got better. A few days later while this book was in progress, one of my friends—no joke—asked me how I liked Kentucky. "I've never been there," I said. "Sure you have," she persisted, "when Father Baptist sent you." This was spooky. I wasn't about to ask her if she also thought of me as being "crotchety" and "dour."

In any case, after a long period of "writer's block," I sat down to begin this novel on Sunday, September 13th. I was depressed, tired, and didn't expect to write anything worth keeping. Suddenly, the words began flying out of my fingers. I've never written a whole novel in under six months, but to my utter amazement I completed this book in only eleven days, and had already outlined the plot for another! This I cannot explain, but I thank God for cracking the dam and granting me a burst of inspiration. I am content.

I have been asked about Father Baptist. Several readers have noted a certain lack of detail about his features, other than references to his threadbare cassock. This I did on purpose, hoping my readers would picture him as they might.

There was, in fact, a real Father John Baptist who did me an important favor once. He was an Irishman, a Capuchin, and a scholar who had studied in Rome. He taught at the Catholic high school I attended many years ago. The students nicknamed him "Sea Dog" because of his habit of assigning us pointless busywork so he could step outside the classroom and spend the bulk of the hour strutting back and forth like a captain on a rocking deck, chain-smoking furiously, his red alcohol-swollen nose bobbing to and fro. I think the post-Vatican II "changes" had caused him enormous internal turmoil, and he wasn't handling it very well.

My older brother, Jim, died during the summer between my freshman and sophomore terms, and my father called the school requesting that one of the friars say the Requiem, loathing as he did the local pastor. But, Dad was informed by the tactless vice-principal, all the priests at the high school were "on vacation" and were therefore "unavailable"—a piece of information Dad did not receive graciously. Driven by impulses I did not fully comprehend—I was fifteen at the time—I took it upon myself to go to the school, enter the cloister, commandeer a seat in the kitchen, and proceeded to cry my guts out into a glass of beer.

Father Baptist, whose roly-poly appearance was perhaps more akin to G. K. Chesterton's Father Brown than Ellis Peters' Brother Cadfael, happened to come lumbering through the galley, his breath heavy with the fumes of aged Irish whiskey. Upon hearing my plight, he immediately canceled his trip to San Francisco and promised to say the Mass for my brother. "In Latin, Father," I begged him. "Please say it in Latin." To this he agreed, surely knowing that it would spark the ire and consternation of his fellow friars who had all abandoned Tradition in favor of Modernism.

That Requiem Mass, celebrated in black vestments, was the last Latin Mass I would attend for twenty years—not because I didn't want to, but because it was banished by the hierarchy. It escapes me how those sworn to protect our souls would have thought this course of action to be a fulfillment of their vows.

After my graduation, Father Baptist left the order, married, became a widower, and apparently died a recluse, refusing admittance to all visitors. Personally, I hope and pray for his final Salvation, if only because of that one brave favor he granted me, a gift I will treasure to my dying day. I honor his muddled memory by giving his name to the central character in my mystery novels, but I draw no other parallels between the two. The Father Baptist at St. Philomena's, in all other respects, is a priest I have yet to meet in real life.

As for my Saint Valeria, the inquisitive reader will not find her in any of the source books mentioned in my tale. She is an amalgam of several historical Virgin Martyrs of the early Church, and is the Patron Saint only of the mythical Archdiocese of Los Angeles in my story, which, as I've said before, bears no resemblance to the real City of Angels located in Southern California. Any similarity between the characters and events in Morley Fulbright's domain and those within any diocese in the United States is completely coincidental. I refer my readers back to the opening paragraph of this introduction.

In conclusion, may I meld myself with a great Saint in his superbly-worded request:

> Devout reader, should this work, as I trust it will, prove acceptable to you, I beg that you will recommend me to the Blessed Virgin, that she may give me great confidence in her protection. Ask this grace for me; and I promise you, whoever you may be, that I will ask the same for you who do me this charity. O blessed are they who bind themselves with love and confidence to these two anchors of salvation, Jesus and Mary. Certainly, they will not be lost.
>
> —Saint Alphonsus Liguori
> *The Glories of May*

Thank-you, and now, on with our tale.

—WLB3

N.B.: Something else requires clarification. The above introduction was written in 1998, several years before the catastrophic event commonly referred to as "Nine Eleven." It is now the year 2005 as we prepare for publication. Since the destruction of the World Trade Center, the "airport experience" has changed significantly. Friends of travelers may no longer accompany them beyond the security station to make their farewells at the departure gate. I realize, as I review the manuscript, that a major scene near the end could not possibly happen in the present world. I have decided, however, not to bring the story "up to date" for two reasons. First, I miss the inherent casualness that used to be an integral part of traveling. The anxiety of the voyage has only been exacerbated by heightened security. Second, this story is a fiction. I am just as entitled to create the kind of airport I wish as I am to place it in the mythical City of Los Angeles, which is itself a fabrication. My license as author to create characters in the mills of my imagination surely extends to the circumstances in which they operate. I hope this will not distract my readers unduly.

Yes, my Friends, I did indeed write *The Search for Saint Valeria* in only eleven days. During that time I was teaching my regular classes at the university and even found time to devour a Perry Mason novel. I read somewhere that Erle Stanley Gardner averaged two weeks to produce a book. The same with Rex Stout. What a remarkable experience it was to witness myself doing that very thing. It was a blip on the screen, I'm afraid, because since then my writing has resumed its usual unwieldy pace. No matter. I thank God for the remarkable if fleeting experience.

Saturday, November Eleventh

**Feast Day of Saint Martin of Tours
Born in Hungary, uncle of Saint Patrick,
Raiser of the dead (397 AD)**

My Namesake's Feast Day!!

1

"YOU MISSED IT," SAID THE PRIEST, finger poised above the tattered Bible on his lap.

"What?" asked the gardener, looking again at the page of his own moth-eaten Douay-Rheims translation. "What did I miss?"

"Recite the verse from Deuteronomy again," instructed the priest.

"Chapter six, verse five," quoth the gardener: "'Thou shalt love the Lord thy God with thy whole heart, and with thy whole soul, and with thy whole strength.'"

"Now read the lawyer's reply to Jesus in Saint Luke's Gospel."

"Chapter ten, verse twenty-seven: 'Thou shalt love the Lord thy God with thy whole heart, and with thy whole soul, and with all thy strength, and—' Ah, I see what you mean. The lawyer added something of his own: 'with all thy mind.'"

"Exactly. And what does this tell us?"

"Hm," said the gardener, rubbing his chin thoughtfully. He was suddenly distracted when something plopped into the ivy next to his feet.

The priest was Father John Baptist. The gardener was yours truly, Martin Feeney. The place was the garden between Saint

Philomena's Church and the rectory. The time was ten o'clock, and it was a beautiful Saturday morning. After all the miserable weather the previous month, it was a joy to sit in the crisp autumn air, smelling the flowers and basking in the sunshine.

Father was sitting on a wooden bench facing the statue of Saint Thérèse the Little Flower. I was resting my weight on the rim of the cement birdbath, its pillar recently reset in cement by none other than Monsignor Michael K. Havermeyer after it had been knocked over by Chief Montgomery "Bulldog" Billowack, who sprained his ankle in the process. My perch, up until just a moment ago, had been shared by the little porous stone bird who, having been broken off long ago and never properly repaired, was forever falling off the edge into the ivy.

"Here, little one," I grunted, easing myself onto my haunches and retrieving my sedimentary avian friend. Gripping my cane, I hauled myself back up onto the rim and set the bird in its proper place at my side.

"So?" said Father patiently.

"So," I said, gathering my thoughts again. "It would seem the lawyer 'enhanced' the Scripture just a tad to suit his purpose. I don't suppose there was much he could do with the next line: 'and thy neighbor as thyself.'"

"Oh, but there was," said Father. "If you turn to the nineteenth chapter of Leviticus, starting at verse sixteen ... Martin?"

My attention was distracted again, this time by a sound—the distinct, unsteady clopping of high heels on the uneven brick path. It's one of those sounds, as you know, for which every man seems to have built-in sonar. I turned my head to see the approaching feet and froze. The shoes were *red,* and they were attached to a pair of shapely legs—legs that were bisected by the most beautiful set of female fulcra I had ever seen.

GARDENING TIPS: It has often been said
that the eye is the mirror of the soul.
True. But as my sagacious dad used to
point out, "The knee is the fulcrum of the
leg." Dad, you see, was a "philoful-
crapher," a predilection inherited by his
son, Martin.

                              --M.F.

N.B. Yes, Mom had great fulcra. Count on
it.

"Oh," I said, struggling to my feet. I was looking at the
woman I wanted to marry, right there in the garden, Father
Baptist presiding. Her dress, too, was red; and she was one of
those rare women on whom red was not an announcement, a
dare, a tease, a lure, an exaggeration, or a come-on, but rather
a simple statement of fact. Red was her color. It looked good
on her.

"Excuse me," she said, her long brown hair flowing grace-
fully around her face and splashing over her shoulders. Her
highlights, too, were—you guessed it—red.

"Um," I said, swallowing my lower jaw. Yes, yes, I knew it
would never work out: me without any visible means of support, she carrying herself with obvious confidence, self-
reliance, ambition, and acumen; she being a cultured pearl and
me being an uncouth mothball; me being twenty years closer
to the Apocalypse than she. All this I understood, even
though I'd never laid eyes on her before. I also knew that I
wanted to spend the rest of my life with her. The details we
could work out along the way.

"I'm looking for Father Baptist," she said, slowing to a
stop.

"You've found him," said Father, rising from the bench
and extending his hand. "And you are—?"

"Sybil Wexler," she smiled, accepting his hand, and not
with that pseudo-equal muscle-pumping grip that many
women are so fond of these days, but rather as a gentle, defer-
ential, sweetly feminine gesture.

"Miss Wexler," beamed Father, "at last we meet."

"Yes," she laughed. "Here's my card as a memento of the
occasion. We always seem to just be voices on a phone, or
initials on a memo. I'm so glad to finally see you."

"Indeed, indeed."

"I trust your wound is healing," she said, referring to Father's right shoulder. "I heard that you were shot."

"The bullet merely grazed me," said Father, rubbing the
spot thoughtfully with his left hand. "It smarted for a week
or so, but I'm fine now. Allow me to present my associate,
Martin Feeney."

"I've heard a lot about you, Mr. Feeney," said she to me,
the sound of her words swirling around my head like swallows

circling the Mission San Juan Capistrano. "I understand that
you're Father Baptist's right-hand man."

"Martin," I managed to say around the obstruction in my
mouth—my tongue and my tie had gotten themselves tangled
into a "reverse double-Windsor." Nodding stupidly, I shook
her hand, then I shook it some more. "Please call me Martin."

"Only if both of you will call me Sybil," said she, turning
her head back toward Father, her hair whirling behind.

In that simple action of her head and hair, the whole sce-
nario of "Martin and Sybil" whirled past my eyes: the love,
the tenderness, the hopes, the dreams, the wedding, the hon-
eymoon, the in-laws, the pregnancy, the birth, the midnight
feedings, the diaper service, the in-laws, the pregnancy, the
birth, the in-laws, the pregnancy, the birth of twins, the in-laws
... Yes, it all went roaring by; and when I snapped back into
focus I remembered why I had never married, and probably
never would. Still ... she was gorgeous.

"Agreed," said Father, motioning for her to sit beside him
on the bench. "And what can I do for you?"

"Official business," she said, digging a small spiral notebook and fountain pen out of her purse. "I need information, and I think you're the one who can give it to me."

"Police business?" asked Father.

"Yes," she nodded, uncapping the pen. "As you know, I
used to work for Homicide Division attached to the County
Coroner's Office. Now I'm in Burglary."

"I'm surprised," said Father. "Why Burglary?"

"It was the farthest place Chief Billowack could think to
transfer me without firing me outright."

"Oh," said Father, a whole tone lower. "A disciplinary
measure."

"You might say that," said Sybil.

"What made Monty mad enough to do that?"

"You."

"Me?"

"Well, something you asked me to do." She hefted her
right fulcrum over the left and settled against the backrest.
"Remember that suicide note you asked me to photocopy?"

"The Buckminster Turnbuckle incident," said Father.
"You gave the copy to Sergeant Wickes."

"And he gave it to you," she said. "And you gave it to
Cardinal Fulbright."

"Did I?" said Father, thinking back.

"You did," I nodded, resuming my awkward place on the edge of the birdbath. After all, I'm Father Baptist's unofficial chronicler. It's my unofficial job to remember such details. "You shoved it to him across the conference table in his office." I turned to her. "It was what you'd call an emotionally charged moment."

"I'll bet," she said. "But I'll wager it was nothing compared to the hour I spent in Chief Billowack's office after the cardinal passed it on to him."

"Oh," gulped Father. "I'm sorry it got you into trouble."

"That it did," she said, but without a hint of further accusation. "Actually, I'm glad for the change. I was never particularly happy about being typecast in the role of a forensics assistant. There are other branches of police work that are less gruesome, and in some ways more interesting. For example, I was immediately assigned to a newly formed task force dealing with the theft of religious objects—which is why I'm here. I'm not a Catholic, and I confess my knowledge of these things is sparse."

Not a Catholic, I mused. Well then, there wouldn't have been grounds for much of a relationship right off the bat. Of course, conversion was a regular part of our parish work, but it's something I've always considered best achieved free from emotional entanglements. On the other hand, God moves in mysterious ways. Then again ...

"I was unaware," Father was saying, "that there has been a rise in the theft of religious objects. In fact, I would have assumed, in light of current trends of thought on the subject, that the issue would be almost moot."

"Indeed," I added, "in the rampant move toward 'renovation,' a lot of Catholic churches have been ridding themselves of their old trappings."

"Yes," she said, "which confuses me, let me tell you. The antique shops are full of discarded Catholic accouterments: tabernacles, altar bells, vestments, you name it. I would have thought that these artifacts would have been turned over to museums."

"Museums wouldn't pay for such things," said the gardener. "And the clerical renovators would prefer cash."

"True," she said, turning her golden brown eyes on me. "Which confuses me even more."

"Not if you understand the underlying impetus of Modernism," I said. "It's what's known as a 'loss of Faith.'"

"So, Sybil," said Father, "how can we help you? What information do you need? And why?"

"The why will have to keep for the present," she said, flipping open her notebook. "What I need at the moment is a clear understanding of 'relics.'"

"Indeed," said Father. "What, may I ask, is your religious background, Sybil?"

"My father was a Unitarian," she answered. "In fact, he used to brag that he was a 'fallen-away' Unitarian."

"Not very far to fall," mumbled the gardener. "And to what?"

"My mother," continued Miss Wexler, tossing me a curious glance, "was a sort of an 'anything goes' Christian. She used to tell me the Bible was full of 'truth stories,' tales that explained moral insights, but that they weren't supposed to be accepted as 'true' in and of themselves."

"Hm," said Father. "That's not much of a background on which to base an understanding of the Catholic veneration of relics. Where can I possibly begin?"

"Why not at the beginning?" suggested Sybil Wexler.

"That would take days," said the gardener. "You could go all the way back to the traditions that surround Genesis, and the preservation of Adam's skull by his descendants."

"Really," she said, setting fountain pen to notebook.

"Yes," said Father. "Extra-Biblical sources say the skull was placed aboard Noe's ark, and later buried by one of Noe's children in a place which the Babylonians called 'Golgotha,' the 'place of the skull.'"

"You mean the place where Jesus was crucified?" she said, eyebrows halfway up her forehead.

"Indeed," said Father.

"You're not joking," she said.

"Not at all," said Father. "The spot is still marked and venerated to this day—though our detractors deny all vehemently. But perhaps we're starting too far back. I suspect your inquiry with respect to relics would have more to do with those of Catholic Saints, relics which were venerated for generations and which have been recently discarded by the modern clergy."

"True," she said. "I'm torn now because I'd like to hear everything, and you've opened up a considerable line of inquiry. I've got a pressing appointment shortly. Perhaps, to save time, you could begin by explaining the difference between a 'first class' relic and one that is 'second class.'"

"Certainly," said Father, closing his Bible and slipping it within the mysterious folds of his cassock. "A 'first class' relic is a piece of the Saint himself."

"You mean a piece of bone," said Sybil.

"Yes," said Father, "or a strand of hair. In some cases it can be the entire body, or any part thereof. The head of Saint Catherine, for example, is preserved in a gilded copper case in Siena. The shoulder of Saint Christopher resides in Saint Peter's in Rome—"

"I thought he wasn't a Saint anymore," interrupted Sybil, frowning. "Sergeant Wickes told me there wasn't enough evidence that he existed so he was de-canonized back in the sixties."

"Sergeant Wickes," said Father, "is hardly an expert on Catholic Tradition. There is plenty of evidence that Saint Christopher existed."

"If he didn't," interjected the gardener, "then whose shoulder is preserved in Rome?"

"Good question," said Sybil. "Of course, I've heard—through Sergeant Wickes and others—that most relics are probably fraudulent."

"Some relics," corrected Father, "undoubtedly are, but not most. There are procedures for authentication, but even so, the prevailing opinion these days is that such things are unimportant, so I hardly think that this is the time for a booming trade in underground relics—which would make *counterfeit* relics a thing of the past, would it not?"

"One would assume so," said Sybil. "But before I comment, what about 'second class' relics?"

"Martin?" said Father, motioning toward me.

"Oh," I said, authoritatively shifting my cane from one hand to the other, "that would be an object that was touched by the Saint. A piece of his habit if he was a monk, a page of a missal, that sort of thing."

"Not so important then," said Sybil.

"No and yes," said Father. "In the Acts of the Apostles, pieces of cloth touched by Saint Peter cured people of illness. Similar miracles have accompanied objects touched by Saint Francis of Assisi and even Padre Pio in recent years."

"Saint Pio of Pietrelcina," said the gardener under his breath, using the good padre's canonized name, "pray for us."

"How about a chalice?" she asked.

"If the Saint in question were a priest or a bishop, certainly," said Father. "Perhaps if you would tell me what it is you're investigating, I could be of more help. I feel that I owe you—"

"You do," smiled Sybil, putting the cap on her pen and closing her notebook. "And though I must press on right now, I'll get back to you when I need more information."

"This wouldn't have anything to do with what's happening this morning, would it?" asked the gardener.

"What do you mean?" asked Sybil, slipping her notebook into her red purse.

"Cardinal Fulbright," said Father, "has ordered the transfer of the relics of Saint Valeria from her resting place under the high altar in the cathedral to the mausoleum at New Golgotha Cemetery."

"It's one more step," I added, "in his plan to tear down the old cathedral so he can build a modern monstrosity in its place."

"You don't know that for sure," said Father.

"It's an educated guess," I countered. "He's been making noises about tearing down the old cathedral for months now. The historical societies have blocked him so far, but he's bound and determined. I think removing the relics of the namesake of the cathedral is just another step in his plan to undermine their arguments. Why keep Saint Valeria's Cathedral standing if she isn't even there?"

"Sounds possible," said Sybil, "but would a prelate of the Catholic Church do such a thing?"

"I wouldn't put it past him," admitted Father. "He has styled himself as a 'champion of change,' and he has made a number of public expressions of his desire to build a new cathedral. We'll just have to wait and see."

"Why don't you join us?" I said, smiling at Sybil. "We're planning to accompany Saint Valeria to her new resting place shortly. There will be a modest ceremony at her re-interment. We're going with a group of friends, an interesting bunch. Since you're interested in relics, there's a wonderful story behind Saint Valeria, and—"

"I wish I could," said Sybil, rising to her feet and snapping her purse shut. "But I'm working on this case."

Father was on his feet instantly. It took me a couple of seconds, struggling against my spinal arthritis.

She waited patiently, then shook Father's hand. "I shouldn't say anything, Father Baptist, but I suspect that you're going to be receiving a call from the cardinal's office some time soon. Perhaps this afternoon."

"Why?" asked Father. "And how do you know?"

"I'm your proverbial fly on the wall," she said to him while she absently shook my hand. She glanced at her watch. "And I must flee if I want to be one jump ahead of the fly-swatter. Good-bye."

With that she went clip-clopping down the brick path, the red of her dress quickly absorbed by the overgrown greenery in the garden.

"Pick it up, Martin," said Father, settling back on his bench.

"Pick up what, Father?" I looked to see if the stone bird had fallen into the ivy again. No, it was still perched on the cement birdbath.

"Your lower jaw," said Father, smiling. "It's sitting on your right shoe."

"Oh, that."

2

"*PIE JESU DOMINE*," sang the Tumblars in meticulously re-hearsed unison, their solemn male voices rumbling through the marble arches of the mausoleum. "*Dona eis requiem. Amen.*"

"Gentle Lord Jesus," whispered the gardener who had been following the translation of the *Dies Irae* in his missal, "grant them rest. Amen."

Roberto Guadalupe, former gravedigger but presently cus-todian of the Del Agua Mission, and his companions, Duggo and Spade, slowly rose to their feet, patting dust from their pants legs. They had just finished cementing a two-foot square slab of marble in place over the slightly smaller hole in the wall, sealing the coffin of Saint Valeria within the lowest niche in the alcove.

Our young friends, the Knights Tumblar as they called themselves, were standing in a semicircle around the cemetery workmen. Their names were, in ascending order of age: Joel Maruppa, Jonathan Clubb, Edward Strypes Wyndham, Pierre Bontemps and Arthur von Derschmidt. This being an impor-tant occasion, they were all attired in morning coats, cravats, waistcoats, striped pants, spats, and patent leather shoes. Each held his opera hat in the crook of his left arm. I might add that theirs was not rented apparel, since they managed to attend enough momentous occasions to warrant owning their own formalwear.

"Well, muchachos, I guess that is it," said Roberto, wiping wet grout from his right hand with a handkerchief he usually wore around his neck.

"What about a plaque?" asked Joel.

"That's right," said Edward. "You can't just leave her behind a blank slab of marble, and so close to the floor."

"This," said Roberto, avoiding their eyes, "is not for me to say. The cardinal, he say nothing about a plaque."

"How is anyone going to know she's here?" asked Arthur.

"This I do not know," shrugged Roberto sadly.

"But she's the Patron Saint of the Archdiocese!" protested Jonathan.

"True," said Pierre Bontemps, sadly wiping his monocle on his sleeve, "which makes her passé." He plugged the lens back into his left eye socket and added, "You gentlemen noticed, did you not, the long procession of the faithful who accompanied our beloved Patroness from the cathedral to this dismal place?"

His sarcasm was not wasted on the ten of us who were present. We constituted, after all, the entirety of that long procession. The Tumblars and Father had acted as pallbearers, transporting the simple but weighty lead coffin from its place under the high altar at Saint Valeria's Cathedral to a rented hearse, and again from the hearse to this secluded alcove deep within the forgotten recesses of the mausoleum. Cardinal Fulbright, having issued the orders that set all this in motion, had not bothered to attend himself.

"There should be at least a simple sign here," said Arthur. "HERE LIES SAINT VALERIA, VIRGIN AND MARTYR. DIED: 363 AD."

The gardener stood somewhat apart, head down, uselessly swinging a censer. "For what it's worth," he whispered, "we apologize."

"And *we* will not forget you," said Pierre, dropping to a crouch. With chivalric determination he pulled a gold ring from his finger and carefully placed it on the narrow top edge of the marble facing stone. "The marker by which we will find you again. Your servant, m'Lady."

"M'Lady," said they all, bowing toward the crypt.

"It's still an outrage," said Joel, back to the issue at hand.

"Sí," sighed Duggo, "but what can we do?"

"Not much, apparently," grumbled Arthur.

Just then I heard the faint sound of footsteps. They seemed to be approaching, but it was hard to tell with all the echoes in that place.

"It would not be out of character," said Father Baptist, "for you Tumblars to hold a series of all-night vigils."

"You mean here?" asked Joel.

"Where else?" asked Father.

Joel looked at Jonathan, who peered at Edward, who glanced at Arthur, who grimaced at Pierre. Then the looks went back around the other way. This seemed odd, considering some of the adventures in which these gentlemen had taken part since their acquaintance with Father Baptist and yours truly. Certainly a night in a mausoleum would be child's play for the likes of them. Yet the looks kept going back and forth, like a moth caught within the safety screen of a camping lantern.

"Perhaps," said Pierre after several seconds. "Or ..."

"Or what?" asked the gardener, curiosity roused.

"Certainly not tonight," said Arthur. "My sister, Beth, is arriving at LAX this afternoon around five, and I promised her a resounding Tumblar welcome."

"I didn't know you had a sister," said Father.

"She's ... not well," said Arthur, fidgeting with his cravat. He seemed embarrassed. "Severe narcolepsy. She lives with my parents in Cleveland. She can't hold a job, you see. Mom and Dad have arranged for her to see a specialist in Italy—of all places—and I'm going to accompany her next week to make sure she arrives at Dr. Zaiden's clinic safely. I'll miss a few days' work, but my parents just aren't up for such a trip, and Beth can't go on a long flight alone, especially to a foreign country. She might start having spells just when she's going through customs or something. In any case, I invited her to come here to enjoy a couple of days with my friends before we go."

"And a Tumblar welcome she shall have," said Pierre. "Of this you can be sure."

"So we can hardy expect her to spend her first night in Los Angeles here in a crypt," said Jonathan.

"This is no place for a lady," said Edward.

"Indeed not," agreed Pierre, looking sadly at the blank slab near the floor.

"Narcolepsy?" asked the gardener. "What's—?"

"What in blazes?!?!" exploded an unexpected voice from the next chamber.

We all turned to see a couple of hands swatting furiously at a mesh of cobwebs that had impressed themselves upon the face of a man in black.

"Oh no," said the gardener. "Not him."

"Monsignor Aspic," said Father Baptist, stepping toward the blur of arms and trailing webs. "What brings you here?"

"Ptui!" sputtered Conrad J. Aspic, advisor, counselor, and gopher for none other than Morley Psalmellus Cardinal Fulbright, Archbishop of Los Angeles. "I say, ptui!"

"Probably," said Pierre under his breath, "the most honest thing he's said in months."

"Let me help you," said Father Baptist, peeling away some of the webbing from the monsignor's chubby face. A particularly gnarly wad of spider silk had affixed itself to an ornate black enamel Crucifix with a golden Corpus dangling from the monsignor's neck by a glistening silver chain.

"Nasty things, spiders," spat Aspic, wiggling his fingers as he tried unsuccessfully to fling the strands to the floor.

"He should know," mumbled Arthur.

Father Baptist seared us all to silence with a sweep of his penetrating eyes. "We are of course pleased that the cardinal has seen fit to send a representative to observe these proceedings."

"Oh that," said the monsignor, uselessly flicking some more strands in the direction of Saint Valeria's unmarked tomb. "No, I'm here on other business."

"We should have—" blurted the gardener, who was then treated to a second dose of Father Baptist's eyes. He added almost inaudibly, "—known."

"And what business is that?" asked Father, clearing his throat for our benefit.

"I went to your rectory first," said Monsignor Aspic, assembling his dignity as best he could, considering the cobwebs which still clung to his ears. "Your housekeeper—"

"Millie," said Father Baptist helpfully.

"Insufferable woman," said the monsignor with a grimace.

"But we love her," said the gardener.

"She told me you would be here," finished Aspic, wiping his forehead with a white silk handkerchief. All this maneuver accomplished was the rolling of the webbing into crests and ridges along his polished hairline.

"And here we are," said Father Baptist, "though I can't imagine what the cardinal would want with me."

"He wants you," spat Aspic angrily, "and that should be enough."

"Of course," said Father, nodding with exaggerated humility.

"I mean—" Suddenly the monsignor seemed to catch himself. Tucking his wrinkled handkerchief into his pocket, he quickly rearranged his face into the mask of largesse and dignity which he normally presented to an unsuspecting world. Indeed, he seemed to take this action a step farther, warping his cheeks and eyebrows into a semblance of cherubic charity and utopian tolerance that I'd never seen there before. It was quite a retrofit.

"I mean," he tried again, this time all grace and fluff, "your shepherd has need of your assistance, Father Baptist. And as you've been of exceptional service to His Eminence in the past, it is hoped that you can exercise your talents on his behalf yet again."

"I still haven't been paid for the last two times," said Father Baptist, his mouth smiling but his eyes not.

"A clerical oversight," assured Monsignor Aspic. "Nothing more. Surely you can understand that with all the complications of late in the Chancery Office, some things have simply slipped through the cracks."

"Like a plaque for this crypt," interjected the gardener.

Father Baptist turned and held me with those unnerving eyes of his that seemed to whisper, accusing yet amused, "Here we go again, my friend, another leap from the pan into the fire." Exhaling slowly, he took the censer from me and handed it to Joel. Without another glance at the other Tumblars, nor even a glance at Monsignor Aspic who was now rocking pleasantly on his soles and jingling the change in his pockets, Father took my arm and said, "Let's go, Martin."

3

"THERE!" BARKED THE CARDINAL, wearily rubbing the purple bump on his forehead with his right hand while pointing frantically with his left. "See for yourself! This is a sacrilege! An outrage!!"

GARDENING TIPS: Considering what we had
witnessed at New Golgotha Cemetery just
minutes before, I guess Cardinal Fulbright
was better able than any of us to explain
"sacrilege" and "outrage." Of course, his
definition was unique to him ...
                                    --M.F.

Father Baptist turned his attention from his lawful superior, who had not even offered his precious sapphire ring for our servile osculation, to the mahogany display case set against the north wall of Cardinal Fulbright's private chapel. Each shelf was protected by a panel of thick, green-tinted glass. Behind the glass, under craftily hidden fluorescent lights, swam an assortment of gold and silver objects, some large, some small, all resting on velvet cushions artistically draped with crimson silk. Next to each treasure was a small typewritten card explaining the precious object and giving a brief history.

"And what, precisely, is missing, Your Eminence?" asked Father.

"Can't you see?" shouted the cardinal. "Right there in the middle of the center shelf. Two golden chalices!"

"Ah," said Father, eyeing the vacant spots that had suddenly become obvious. Two typed cards stood guard over circular impressions in the silk, indentations from which two sacred vessels had been removed. "And when did you first notice that they were missing?"

"Early this morning," huffed the cardinal, rubbing his bump harder and harder. "I came in here after breakfast to collect my thoughts, and there they were—gone!"

GARDENING TIPS: My reader might be interested in knowing that the bump Cardinal
Fulbright kept rubbing throughout the conversation had a history. He got it falling off a speaking platform, or rather
just after the fall. It might even pique
your curiosity further to learn that Father Baptist tackled and fell with him for
the express purpose of getting him off
that very platform.
    The cardinal's parting words of thanks
to Father Baptist for performing this

unique and somewhat unorthodox service
upon his person: "Out! Get out of my
sight, and don't ever approach me, not on
any pretext, ever again. Do you hear me?
Out! Out!! Out!!!"

                                        --M.F.

N.B. The fact that the cardinal had ordered Father back into his august presence
after all that commotion (and more since)
will tell you how much the stolen property
meant to him.

"And when was the last time you noticed them?" asked
Father. "I mean, when can you be sure that they were
here—?"

"I know what you mean," barked Fulbright, tucking his
arms behind his back and starting to pace. "Let me see. The
last time Bishop Bonsignore, the papal nuncio, came to
visit—when was that, Monsignor?"

Monsignor Aspic, who had been preening the last of the
cobwebs from his hair in front of a full-length mirror at the
opposite wall, turned and smiled with overflowing patience
and understanding. As he did so, I noticed he had surrepti-
tiously slipped his ornate pectoral Crucifix into the pocket of
his black clerical shirt, leaving the chain to waddle tellingly
beneath his chins. "Wednesday. Three days ago. As Your
Eminence will recall, he was here to discuss with you the matter of—"

"Yes, yes," huffed the cardinal. "He was here. That's the
point. I remember bringing him in to show him my collection
that evening after dinner."

"That would have been around nine-thirty," added the
monsignor. "Then you had brandy in the—"

"Yes, yes," hissed the cardinal. "It was nine-thirty."

"And you don't remember seeing the chalices since then?"
asked Father.

"Not precisely," said the cardinal. "Aspic, have you—?"

"Oh no, Your Eminence," said Monsignor Aspic, walking
buoyantly toward us. "I haven't had cause to notice. I don't
believe I've even been in here since that night."

"So the theft could have taken place any time," said Father
Baptist, "during the last three days. I suggest that you call the

police, Your Eminence. I understand that Burglary Division has just instituted a task force—"

"Yes, yes, yes," growled Morley Fulbright, pacing more wildly. "I know all about that. I did call them, and a couple of policemen came and dusted for prints this morning. But that Wexler woman was with them, and I don't trust her."

Father and I exchanged glances.

"And what do you want me to do?" asked Father.

"Why, to find my chalice!" snarled Fulbright, stopping in his tracks. "What the Hell did you think I brought you here for?"

"Just one chalice?" asked Father. "I thought you said there were two—"

"One is just an old relic," spat the cardinal. "It's of questionable authenticity and is of no possible consequence. But the other, that was a gift from Professor Murkenstein, my mentor from the university. That one holds deep significance for me."

"Hm," said Father, bending to study the metal lock on the glass panel. "There are tiny scratches here around the keyhole. It's possible that the lock was picked."

"Of course it was picked," huffed Fulbright. "No one has the key but me."

"Did the policemen find fingerprints?"

"Yes. Mine."

"No one else's?"

"No. But thieves have been known to wear gloves."

"Indeed." Father straightened, but continued his examination of the shelves and their contents. "I notice four other cards without accompanying artifacts—"

"Yes, yes," said the cardinal. "Reliquaries, insignificant trifles."

"Did they contain relics?"

"Yes, yes. Dubious things, not important. None of your concern."

"They are if they were stolen at the same time as the chalices. Were they?"

The cardinal scrunched his lips into something resembling a cauliflower. It must've hurt. "Apparently."

"And this upper shelf on the right," said Father, "it looks as though there used to be a number of large objects here, but there are no cards, and no—"

"Old monstrances, a Spanish ciborium, and a few other odds and ends," said the cardinal with obvious distaste. " I sold them some time ago, and they're beside the point. They're none of your concern."

"I see," said Father.

"Good," said the cardinal.

"These cards in here," said Father, continuing his perusal of the shelves, "they all look the same. Who typed them?"

"Bishop Ravenshorst," said the cardinal, resuming his frantic pacing. "Our archdiocesan historian—recently deceased, as you well know."

GARDENING TIPS: Bishop Jeremiah Ravenshorst, as we knew too well, died of severe electrocution the previous June in the Chapel of Saint Barbara, Patroness of Artillery, Explosives, and Lightning. It's a long story, and one which, along with all this poor gardener's literary attempts, has yet to be published.
                                        --M.F.

"Could I possibly have these two cards that went with the chalices?" asked Father.

"Oh, I don't see why not," snarled the cardinal, fumbling among his red robes. Red, in this gardener's opinion, was not really his color.

"Perhaps I'll also take the four cards connected with the relics," added Father.

"Grrrr," grrrred the cardinal, producing a ring brimming with keys.

"And do you have any pictures of the stolen articles?" asked Father as the cardinal pawed at the lock. "Perhaps among the post cards you sell in the gift shop?"

"I don't think so," said Morley as the lock finally gave way amidst the tinkling of keys, and the panel slid back.

"Oh, but there *are* pictures," said the monsignor, nervously fingering the sagging protuberance in his shirt pocket. "In the booklet we include with our guided tours."

"The guided tours don't come back here into my residence," snarled the cardinal, snatching the cards from their velvet nests and pushing them into Father Baptist's hand.

"Um, actually," coughed Monsignor Aspic, "they do, on occasion. Only when you're out of town, of course."

"I wasn't aware of this practice in my absence," said the cardinal coldly, "and it will now cease."

"Of course," said the monsignor, momentarily lowering his eyes.

"You were saying something about a brochure," said Father Baptist.

"Oh yes," said Aspic, recovering his aplomb, blossoming perky and full of wisdom, "I'm quite sure the old chalice—*Le San Pres'que Grall,* I believe it's called—is in the brochure. I think the Murkenstein cup is in there as well, and probably the relics. History and artifacts and all that. I'll go see if I can fetch a copy." With that the monsignor disappeared in a puff of cologne and mouthwash.

"You do understand, Your Eminence," said Father, slipping the cards into the mysterious folds of his cassock without looking at them, "that though my former career was on the police force, burglary was not my field."

"This crime," grumbled Cardinal Fulbright, "is worse than murder. I don't care what it takes, I want the criminal found and my chalice returned."

"Very well," said Father, bowing slightly. "I will do what I—"

"Just bring me my chalice," said the cardinal, turning suddenly and stomping away. "I want my chalice."

4

"I DON'T KNOW HOW to tell you this," said the gardener as he and Father seated themselves in the dining nook back at the rectory. It was precisely noon. "I think His Elegance wants his chalice."

"You may have something there, Martin," smiled Father, unfolding his napkin. I almost couldn't hear him over the clang and clatter of Millie's vicious meal preparation.

"Did you notice," I ventured, "that Monsignor Aspic was wearing the Crucifix you gave him?"

"Indeed I did. Was that only two weeks ago?"

I paused to think. "Less."

"I hadn't expected that he'd wear it in public."

"Considering how repulsed he was when you first handed it to him," I said, rearranging the salt-and-pepper shakers.

"It did save his life, after all."

"For what, I'd like to know," huffed Millie, skewering something wiggly in a pot with her deadly two-pronged fork.

"Did you also notice," I asked, glancing at Millie's silver Crucifix suspended over the sink, "how he kept it out of sight in the cardinal's presence?"

"Hm-hm," nodded Father. "'Unto the monsignor indeed a stumbling block, and unto the cardinal foolishness.'"

"First Corinthians," said I, "one twenty-three—sort of. I wonder what will come of it."

"He's going to be on that God-awful talk show again tonight," snarled Millie.

"What," I asked, "'Religion Revisited'?"

"I'm going over to the Cladusky's to watch it with Muriel after dinner," she shouted between metallic collisions, "in case anyone's interested. They, at least, have a television."

"Let's say Grace, shall we?" said Father Baptist calmly. "In the name of the Father, and of the Son, and of the Holy Ghost ..."

The phone rang just as we said our final "Amen." It started a second chime but stopped in mid-jingle. Even household appliances know when to defer to our Millie's strict schedule at Saint Philomena's.

"I wonder what could have become of Monsignor Havermeyer," said Father as her shadow fell across the tablecloth. "Ah, Millie—"

"Duck!" yelled yours truly as our beloved housekeeptrix slammed our lunch down between us. Everything on the table—glasses, mismatched silverware, chipped coffee cups—rocked, rolled, then quivered to silent attention.

"No, turkey," she snarled. "Same as yesterday and the day before. I'm just working through the carcass."

"And producing a feast every time," slavered the gardener, rubbing his hands together.

"A likely story," said Millie, turning back to the stove.

"And just think, Father," I said, taking up my fork with gusto, "Thanksgiving is just around the corner, and we'll get to do this all over again."

"Don't bet on it," said Millie, bashing a frying pan against a soup kettle for no apparent reason. "Not on my budget."

"I'm not partial to big meals on Thanksgiving anyway," said Father, slicing a piece of white meat with his knife. After transporting a morsel to his mouth, he reached inside his cassock and produced the glossy pamphlet that had been provided by Monsignor Aspic as we departed the cardinal's residence. He spread it flat beside his plate. "Hmm."

"Interesting?" I asked around a wad of steamed broccoli.

"Here's the Murkenstein Chalice," he said, pointing to a glittering cup photographed under bright lights against a blue background.

Even upside-down, as it was from where I sat, it looked gaudy and tasteless—an ostentatious and somewhat angular thing never intended for liturgical purposes, totally unlike the simple but purposeful chalice on the opposite page.

"What's that other one?" I asked.

"The other chalice that was stolen," said Father. He leaned close to read the words. "Monsignor Aspic had it right: *Le San Pres'que Grall.*"

"What's that mean?"

"My French is rustier than I thought," said Father. "'The Holy next to the Grail.' I can't make sense of that."

"Does the pamphlet give an explanation?"

"Hmm. The same as on the typed card: 'An ancient cup which may trace its origin to 1st century Palestine. Presented by the Carmelite Nuns of Port Tobacco, Maryland, to Francis James McInery in 1940 upon his appointment as Archbishop of Los Angeles.' Hardly a comprehensive history."

"Archbishop McInery," I said. "I remember he gave a commencement address at my high school graduation. I think he retired shortly after that."

"He was the last of his kind," said Father, thoughtfully closing the brochure. "By the way, Millie, where's Monsignor Havermeyer?"

"Right here, Father, right here," puffed the monsignor, coming down the hallway toward the kitchen. "I was looking up something in your study when the phone rang. I'm sorry to be late, Millie, but the call sounded im ... por... tant ..."

Monsignor Havermeyer slowed to a halt at the sight of the wedge of dried crust on the plate set before his empty chair. Right in the center of the stale slice of bread was a small, gnarled lump of very dark meat. "Oh, come now, Millie. Have a heart—"

"Exactly," she snapped, banging a couple of pots. "Enjoy."

"I give up," sighed the monsignor, sinking into his chair, wiping a trickle of sweat from his mangled forehead.

GARDENING TIPS: Monsignor Havermeyer's
forehead and hands had been scarred by
flames in the same electrical fire that
killed Bishop Ravenshorst. Write letters
of complaint to every available publisher.
                                    --M.F.

N.B.: I know, I know. If you're reading
this, then it has been published. This is
what comes of writing in a vacuum . . .

"I knew you would," said the gardener. "Who was it?"
"Who was what?" asked Havermeyer, studying the little
muscle on his plate.
"Who was on the phone?"
"Oh that." The monsignor rummaged around in his cassock and produced a piece of notebook paper. He eyed the
squiggled information that had cost him his lunch and crum-
pled it up. "Somebody for you, Father Baptist. Called himself Willie Kapps, I think. He was hard to understand. Said it
was urgent, that you'd know who he was, and that he had to
see you right away."
"Willie," said the gardener. "He's never called here before."
"Indeed," said Father around a piece of turkey meat. "It is
always I who call upon him. Today seems to be a day of
many firsts."
"Such as?" asked Havermeyer, nudging the thing on his
crust with a fork. It was quite dead.
"For one," said Father, "the cardinal wants me to locate
something that was stolen from his residence."
The monsignor set down his fork with a decisive wallop.
"Do you mean to tell me—? But he only drags you in
when—" His eyes narrowed. "Who's dead this time?"
"Four men, actually," said Father, taking a sip of pale wine.
"Among the missing items were several reliquaries. Saints
Athanasius, John Chrysostom, Augustine, and Pope Gregory
the Great. The cardinal didn't seem very concerned about
them. There were also two chalices taken. One is called Le
San Pres'que Grall, about which, again, the cardinal was not
particularly upset. But the other chalice—the reason he
dragged me in—was a gift from his mentor in college."
"Murkenstein," said Havermeyer. "He retired before I was
ordained. An expert in the theology of Paul Tillich."

"Oh," said the gardener. "That explains it."

"Professor Murkenstein presented Morley with that chalice when he was elevated to archbishop," said Havermeyer. " I seem to remember some kind of a ceremony at a Knights of Columbus meeting. I think the old coot died a year or two ago."

"I take it that Professor Murkenstein wasn't one of your faves," observed the gardener, sipping his ginger ale.

"He was at one time," said Havermeyer, closing his eyes for a long second. "Of course, that was before I, uh, started reconsidering things last summer."

"Did Cardinal Fulbright ever use this Murkenstein Chalice at Mass?" asked Father.

"Not that I ever heard," said Havermeyer. "No, I'd wager my lunch—ahem—that it went straight into that trophy case of his."

Suddenly the table grew dark. We looked up to see Millie's fierce eyes glaring down at us. "Are you saying, Father, that the cardinal wants you to go detecting again?"

"I'm afraid so," said Father, voice steady under the circumstances. "Orders are orders."

"You realize that whenever that happens," she rumbled, "things go haywire."

"Yes," said Father, "that seems to follow."

There was a long pause. Even the thing on Monsignor Havermeyer's plate skipped a beat, and it was quite dead, don't forget.

"Good," said Millie, turning back to her stove. "I'm beginning to like it around here."

The thing on the monsignor's crust sighed and rolled over.

"Well," said Havermeyer, tossing down his napkin. " I think I'll mosey over to 'Peanuts' across the street. The Saturday special is pot roast. I suppose you'll want me to cover confessions this afternoon, Father."

"If I'm not back in time, yes," said Father Baptist, smiling his appreciation for the help. Monsignor Havermeyer had only recently joined us. Before that Father Baptist had been entirely on his own when it came to administering the Sacraments.

"What could Willie want?" I asked as the monsignor exited the door to the garden.

"I don't know," said Father, "but I think interesting things are starting to happen."

5

"UH OH," SAID THE GARDENER, as he veered the parish Jeep toward the curb in front of the shop owned and operated by Willie "Skull" Kapps—also known as Guillaume du Crane Cristal, Los Angeles' sole source of mweemuck root tea and seller of rare unmentionables—and I do mean unmentionables. He was also Father Baptist's occasional consultant in matters of the arcane and the occult.

The serpentine street was hard to find, but once I located it and began tracing its length I was bound to see the warped sign swinging from a rusted metal gallows over the doorway. The sign was shaped like a huge, glaring eyeball. The inscription painted across the cornea said: WIDE EYE DO DAT? Another sign nailed crookedly on the door announced:

FORTUNES UNTOLD
∞ BONES READ ∞
POTIONS FOR ALL OCCASIONS
GUILLAUME DU CRANE CRISTAL, PROPRIETOR.

"'Uh oh' is right," said Father Baptist, eyeing the scarecrow-like figure who was hunched at that very door, dreadlocks jiggling, apparently screwing something heavy and metallic into the wood above the elaborate doorknob.

"He sees us," I said, turning off the ignition.

Father Baptist was already shaking Willie's spindly hand by the time I had grunted my way out of the driver's seat.

"Jack the Black," Willie was saying to Father as I approached. "You come. T'ank-you, t'ank-you." When he turned to shake my hand his coconut eyes were too busy glancing nervously up and down the street to look me in the face. "Martin Mon," he rasped like rough sandpaper, "inside, inside."

A bell tinkled as we entered, an irritating sound that penetrated my very being, playing counter-harmonious havoc with my spinal tissues. I made a mental note to record that infernal sound some day and have it analyzed. It defied reason that a single bell could be out-of-tune with itself.

As Willie motioned us through his shop, my eyes darted around the display cases crammed with withered things that had once been alive—things which seemed to pulsate and quiver on the periphery of your vision until you looked directly at them. Talismans and masks cluttered the walls, and the smell of mold and sour ashes permeated the air. This was not your typical magick shop or occult book parlor. Whatever powers resided here, they were primitive, untamed, and unnervingly real.

"You said it was urgent," said Father, coming to a halt near a display of tiny, hand-carved statues.

"Dat Ah did, Mon," said Willie. "An' wot Willie say, he mean."

"We're listening," said Father.

"Willie need to ask dah favor," said Willie, slinking around behind a rickety wooden counter. "No one else can Ah ask." He stooped down out of sight and started rummaging. "No one else Willie can trust." Finding whatever it was he was looking for, he raised himself to his narrow height and set something on the countertop. "Trust wit' dis."

I took a wary step closer to have a look. It was a stained leather pouch about the size of a tuna sandwich, tied at the throat with a soiled yellow cord.

"And what is 'this'?" asked Father, examining the tassel of the cord with the index finger of his right hand.

"Dah trust dat Ah ask," said Willie. He set his hands palms down, fingers spread like dry twigs, on each side of the pouch. "Willie won you keep dis safe."

"I repeat," said Father, moving his fingers over the leather. "What is it?"

"Ah won you keep dis," whispered Willie, "but promise not open, not look inside. An' above all, tell no one."

Father took his hand away. "You ask much, my friend."

"Ah ask because Ah has dah need."

Father glanced at me, noted the expression of warning on my face, and turned his attention back to the anxious proprietor. "Considering my position, Willie, I cannot possess nor carry contraband. That would make me an accessory after the fact, and I can't risk a scandal of that sort."

"Dis not drugs," said Willie, his voice pinched a note higher. "Dis not stolen. It come honestly to me—honest!"

"Then what are you afraid of?" asked Father.

"Afraid?" shivered Willie.

"You have always protected your shop with spells. You and I both know the nature of those incantations. Now we find you installing a deadbolt on the front door. Hardly an act of Faith. You look as though you've lost weight—"

"And for you," noted the gardener, "that can't be easy."

"Now you want me," said Father, "to take this, I assume, within the protection of my Sanctuary."

Willie licked his licorice lips with a dry tongue. The motion sent something slithering in a glass case nearby. Naturally it played dead when I looked to see what it was. Just a swatch of cloth, actually, with strange symbols around the edges.

"Ah ask you trust," said Willie after several long seconds. "As mah fren."

"How long," asked Father, "do you want my trust to last? How long do you want me to keep this thing without knowing what it is?"

"'Til Willie ask for it back."

"And then?"

"An' den Ah t'ank you."

"And then?"

"Den we drink some mweemuck root tea, maybe sip dah homemade gin, an' talk about dah old times."

"And I still won't know what it is?"

Willie sucked in his lips, crunched his eyes, and then let his face snap back into its usual contortions. "We see."

Father turned away to think for a moment.

I turned away, too, not knowing what else to do. I feigned interest in a couple of glittering objects in a case beneath a large casting quilt. Then my interest became genuine. Why, those things were—

"Very well," I heard Father say behind me. "You have my trust, Willie. I pray I won't regret it."

"Ah pray, too," said Willie, sighing gratefully. "Willie pray whole bunch."

"Me, too, O Lord," I whispered in unison with the soft sound of a leather pouch slipping within the mysterious folds of Father's threadbare cassock. I peeled my attention from the shiny objects in the case. "Great God in Heaven, me too."

"Let's go, Martin."

"Sure thing, Father. Sure."

6

"UH OH," SAID THE GARDENER, as Father Baptist and I emerged from the front door of our parish church twenty minutes later.

"Right again," said Father, eyeing the black-and-white police car that had just pulled up to the curb.

"What was that you and Willie were saying about trust?" I asked as a pair of red shoes emerged from the passenger side of the vehicle.

"Perhaps we're about to find out," said Father as the shoes clip-clopped toward us, accompanied by a pair of masculine wingtips. "Good afternoon, Officer Wexler."

"Sybil, Father," she corrected him, ascending the steps toward us. "Why so official all of a sudden?"

"Because this looks official," said Father.

She gave him a penetrating look, then turned her attention to the man beside her. "This is Lieutenant Holcomb who is working with me on a case. Lieutenant Holcomb, Father Baptist."

"My gardener," said Father, indicating none other than, "Martin Feeney."

The man shaking my hand looked as though he had been molded of sopping wet clay and left under a UV lamp to dry. He was fifty or so, balding, with large drooping ears. His suit hung crookedly from his stooped shoulders. "Sergeant Wickes sends his regards," he said with a voice that matched his face.

"Please return them stamped 'appreciated,'" I said. " I didn't catch your first name, Lieutenant."

"Tragg," he said.

"I'm sorry?"

"Tragg."

Apparently Lieutenant Holcomb's parents had read too much Erle Stanley Gardner. Figuring he'd received better comments all his life than I could dig up on the spur of the moment, I said nothing; but boy, I hated to let the opportunity pass.

GARDENING TIPS: Within Gardener's own
mythical city of Los Angeles, Perry Mason
was the lawyer to have defending you
against a murder charge. His principal

```
antagonists, aside from the myopic dis-
trict attorneys, were Sergeant Holcomb and
Lieutenant Tragg. Tragg Holcomb, as you
will see, well, you will see. Don't mind
me if I utilize his names interchangeably.
I just love calling a character in my
story "Tragg."
                                    --M.F.
```

"And what brings you to Saint Philomena's a second time in one day?" asked Father, smiling quizzically at Sybil.

"You've been to see the cardinal?" she asked.

"Yes."

"And?"

"I suspect you know all about it," said Father.

"Enough to guess," she answered.

Father glanced at me.

I glanced at Father.

She wasn't guessing—the cardinal said she'd been there when the police checked for fingerprints. What was her game?

"So," said Father to her, "does the cardinal's problem have something to do with the case you're working on?"

"I suspect it's related. As I told you this morning, there's been a rash of thefts regarding religious articles. Pawnshops, antique shops, auction houses, those sorts of establishments."

"Catholic articles, specifically?" asked Father.

"Well," said Tragg, "they would hardly be Protestant, now would they?"

"Indeed," said Father. "This morning, Sybil, you were primarily concerned with relics."

"Just to get a handle on them," she said. "You must admit that keeping parts of bodies is a bit ... morbid."

"It might seem so," said Father, "if you don't understand the history behind the practice."

"Do you have any here?" asked Tragg. "Relics?"

"Of course," said Father. "Every day I say Mass at the altar in the church. Underneath the altar cloth, right in front of the Tabernacle, is a flat, rectangular stone containing a bone chip of Saint Candidus, who was martyred under the Emperor Maximian in the third century."

"And that doesn't bother you?" asked Sybil.

"Not in the least," said Father. "After all, in the end we're all food for worms. I'm simply a Realist. An Ultra-realist, actually. But surely this is afield of the purpose of your visit."

"Perhaps," said Sybil. "We understand that you paid a visit to the establishment of Guillaume du Crane Cristal a short while ago."

"Alias Willie 'Skull' Kapps," added Tragg.

"And how did you know that?" asked Father.

"I'm just a fly on the wall," said Sybil.

"Why did you go there?" asked Tragg.

"Because he called and asked me to," said Father. "He's a friend."

"A friend?" asked Tragg, eyebrows raised.

Father said nothing.

"Did he try to sell you anything?" asked Sybil.

Father folded his arms across his chest.

"Did you understand the question?" asked Tragg.

"What I don't understand," said Father, "is the purpose of the question."

"That's our concern," said Tragg.

"Mine, too," said Father.

"Just what is the nature of your friendship with this man?" asked Tragg in low, slow tones.

"I might tell you that," said Father, "when you tell me the nature of your concern."

"What are you hiding?" asked Tragg.

"I might ask you the same question," said Father.

"Now see here—"

"Perhaps we're getting off on the wrong foot," interjected Sybil Wexler, trying to sound sweet but nervously so.

"No 'perhaps' about it," mumbled the gardener, ignored as usual. I was getting really creepy feelings about that leather pouch Father had secreted behind a loose stone in the church just moments before. What was going to be the price of Willie's trust?

"Were you aware," said Tragg, "that Willie Kapps went to jail in connection with a seance racket?"

"If you know about that," said Father, "you know that I was the one who arrested him. I was a lieutenant myself at the time."

"And by so doing you cleared him of a murder rap," snapped Tragg.

"And pinned it on the real murderer," said Father.

"Sounds fishy to me," said Tragg.

"What's wrong," asked Father, "with punishing the guilty and exonerating the innocent?"

"I'd hardly call a crook who feeds on gullible widows 'innocent,'" said Tragg.

"He was innocent of *murder*," said Father. "He paid for the lesser crime with two years of his life. Just what are you insinuating, Lieutenant?"

"Oh, I don't know," said Tragg, rubbing his chin. "First you get him off a murder charge, nail him for something relatively minor, and then you wind up being his pal. It just seems to me—"

"Yes," said Father, turning his attention to Sybil. "It would seem that I am wasting your time, Officers." She winced at the cutting formality. "You approached me in the hopes that I could give you information on holy objects, and it is becoming clear that I am not helping you in this regard. Now if you will excuse us, Martin and I must be off about the cardinal's business."

"I'm sorry, Father," said Sybil hastily. "You must forgive my partner. He didn't mean to imply—"

"Words mean what they say," said Father. "And so do I. This interview is concluded."

With that I felt his hand grip my arm and turn me in the direction of the back parking lot. Looking over my shoulder, I saw Sybil whispering angrily and making nasty faces at Tragg. The long-eared lieutenant just shoved his hands deep into his pockets and snorted.

"That could have gone better," I whispered as we walked past the statue of Saint Joseph, the Patron of Departing Souls.

"It's a fallen world," said Father. "Everything could be better, but it isn't."

"How did they know we went to see Willie?"

"Perhaps he's being watched."

"And now we're being watched, too?"

"I wouldn't be surprised."

7

"JACK?" ASKED THE MAN behind the counter. "Is that Jack Lombard? Haven't seen you in years. What's with the get-up? You undercover or something?"

We had just entered a pawnshop near 3rd Street and La Brea.

"Dennis," said Father, touching his Roman collar self-consciously. "It *has* been a while. This isn't a disguise. I resigned some time ago and took up a new profession."

"Well I'll be damned," said the proprietor, slapping his thigh. "If you'd've told me ten years ago that Jack Lombard would end up in a pulpit, I'd've told you where to get off. Catholic, eh? So what am I supposed to call you?"

"Father John Baptist is my religious name."

"Heh, heh. Well okay, uh, *Father* ... But what about Christine? I mean, she, that is—"

"My wife died," said Father. "Cancer." A gray cloud passed briefly behind his eyes, then disintegrated as the light normally residing there regained its composure.

"I'm sorry," said the man, wincing. "She was one heck of a lady. After being married to a woman like that, and then losing her, I guess I can see why you might ... Oh, bosh. What do I know?" He turned his eyes on me. "Who's this, your altar boy?"

"Sometimes," I said.

"Dennis Goodman," said Father, "this is my gardener and occasional altar boy, Martin Feeney."

"Not to mention chauffeur, unofficial chronicler, and cook when Millie's away," I added, shaking Mr. Goodman's hand.

"Anything you say," he said dubiously. "You sure you're not just undercover, Jack? I mean, Father? You know you can trust me."

"That's why I'm here," said Father. "And this collar is for real. Would you mind if I asked you a few questions?"

"Shoot."

"I'm investigating something for the archdiocese. Your name just popped into my mind because you run a pawnshop. It's come to my attention that there have been a number of recent thefts from establishments such as yours, specifically of Catholic religious articles."

"You're telling me. I got ripped off just two days ago."

Father looked surprised. "Really."

"Damn bastard," spat Goodman. "Broke my front window with a brick and snatched a whole bunch of things."

"Like what?" asked Father.

"Like a monsterunce, and a chiburgium, and a—"

"You mean a monstrance and a ciborium?"

"Whatever. Such horrible names for such beautiful things." Mr. Goodman snapped his fingers. "They took everything in the display except this one little thingy—let me see, where did I put it? Oh yeah, here it is. I think it's called a requilary."

He held up a small golden object.

"Reliquary," corrected Father.

"Sure," said Goodman, eyeing the little glass window in the center. "I think it's for storing body parts or something. This one's empty—though whether they didn't take it because of that, or because it's small, or they just didn't see it—who knows?"

"But," said Father, "they did take everything else from the window display?"

"I'll say they did. My insurance guy isn't convinced."

"They never are," said Father. "Tell me, where did you obtain these things that were taken?"

"From Father Upshaw. Catholic I'm not, and why Father Upshaw was so anxious to get rid of them is beyond me."

"Upshaw, you say?"

"He's pastor at Saint Somethingorother's, over on 4th Street."

"I'll find it. You say he was in a hurry?"

"Well, I don't mean like he was shifty-eyed and on the run. It's like, he said something about his church is being renovated, and he had this junk to sell."

"That was his term?"

"Yeah, 'junk.' He had these things I just mentioned, some hand bells, and some great candlesticks. I turned down the vestments—wouldn't know what to do with them. He also had a 'high altar' in the back of his pickup, a humungous thing carved out of solid oak. I told him to try Norman down the street. He supplies stuff like that to the movie studios."

"Hm," said Father. "Did anyone from the parish come by and express interest in the objects in your window?"

"Yeah, several people. One guy in particular got really worked up over the prices I was asking. He said it was an outrage. I told him I simply had to make a profit over what I paid Father Upshaw for the stuff, and that just got him madder."

"Did he happen to leave his name? A business card, perhaps?"

"Come to think of it, he did. Said he'd try to raise the money somehow and wanted me to call him if any other offers were made."

"Were there?"

"What?"

"Other offers made?"

"The things were only on display in the window for an afternoon. That night, crash! All gone. I lost a bundle."

"And did this man ever get in touch with you again?"

"Nope. Here, I think I put his card in the cash register." Mr. Goodman hit the TOTAL/SALE key and the drawer opened with a metallic clang. He slipped out the card, handed it to Father, and shoved the drawer back in with his stomach.

"Hm," said Father, examining the card. "'Archibald Roring, Investment Consultant.' Perhaps we'll pay him a visit."

"You think he might've done it," asked Goodman, "and that's why he never came back?"

"I don't know," said Father, "but I do want to talk to him. Do you happen to know of any other proprietors who experienced similar thefts?"

"Yeah. I belong to an association of pawnbrokers. I can think of three who complained of the same thing at the last meeting."

"Could you give me their names and addresses?"

"Sure."

"By the way, do you happen to know what Father Upshaw did with the vestments?"

"Why?"

"Well," said Father with a shrug, "to tell you the truth, my parish is small and poor. The vestments I have are very old and in need of repair."

"Ah, I see," winked Goodman. "I think Norman told me that he bought them. He's three blocks down on the right. 'Norman's Studio Supply.' I'll give him a buzz and tell him you're coming over, and that you're an old friend of mine."

"Thank-you," said Father. "Martin?"

"Here," I said, detaching myself from the woodwork.

8

"THAT'S WHAT HE SAID," said Norman Slater, pointing to the vestments hanging in plastic shrouds. "'Father Jack is an old friend. Just send me the bill.' He said that if the altar bells hadn't been stolen from his store, he'd've thrown them in, too."

"I don't know what to say," said Father.

"Just say a Mass for him," said Mr. Slater, winking. "Make it several. He's an atheist from way back. Me, I think I've heard of you. Weren't you in the news a few months ago?"

"Unfortunately," said Father. "Martin, would you mind seeing to these vestments? Be careful not to wrinkle them as you put them in the car."

"No problem," I said, taking two off the rack—the green and the red—and heading for the door. On my return trip a minute or so later I heard just a couple of lines:

"So you did buy the altar?"

"Yeah, you wanna see it?"

"In a minute. But first, let me ask you this ..."

I snatched the white and the rose and headed out the front door. When I came back, they were saying:

"Statues, you say? Of which Saints?"

"Well, Father, you know as well as I do that most statues are just products of an artist's imagination. You can't tell who is who just by looking at them."

"Of course you can, Norman. Saints are identified by the things they are holding, or objects at their feet."

"So you wanna see them, too? They're in the back."

"Yes, but let me also inquire about ..."

I left with the gold and the black. Upon my return, there was one set of vestments left. "Hold on," I said aloud.

"What is it?" asked Father.

"This last set is blue," I said, hefting it high by the hanger hook. "You don't see a lot of blue vestments."

"They are a special privilege," said Father, "granted to orders and shrines with a strong Marian devotion. The Franciscan missionaries used to wear them on Our Lady's feast days here in California."

"Hm," I said, heading for the door again. "You learn something new every day. You wouldn't happen to be thinking of starting a strong Marian devotion, would you, Father?"

"You mean a *stronger* devotion than I already have?" he smiled. "Sounds like a good plan."

When I came back, I was puffing. Just walking is hard for me, but carting heavy vestments ... well, no matter. It was Father who would bear the weight at Mass for years to come.

"Martin," said Father. "Mr. Slater is going to show us that altar."

We followed Norman Slater through a door and into a large warehouse. It was a huge building, and it was filled to the ceiling with all kinds of antique and modern furniture, ornate rugs and draperies, chandeliers and lamps, paintings and etchings. You wanted it, Norman had it.

"Here's one of the statues," he said as we came around a corner.

"Saint Philomena," said Father, pleasantly surprised.

"How can you tell?" asked Mr. Slater.

"Martin?"

"The scourging whip in her right hand," I explained, humbled. "The arrows in her left, and the anchor at her feet." I must admit a tear gathered in the corner of my right eye at the sight of our own parish Saint. "I apologize," I said under my breath. This statue was twice as tall, and far more elegant, than the replica that resided in one of the alcoves back home.

"What do all those things mean?" asked Slater.

"Those are the ways the Emperor Diocletian tried to execute her," I said. "She was skinned alive, shot full of arrows, and thrown into the Tiber chained to an anchor."

"But she didn't die?" asked Norman, eyebrows high.

"Not until she was inspired to tell the emperor how to finally kill her."

"And this," said Father, moving swiftly to another, equally stunning form. "This is Saint Lucy."

"The plate in her hands," I indicated, "containing her eyes."

"Urg," gulped Mr. Goodman.

"Saint Martha," said Father, coming to the next statue.

"The dragon at her feet," I explained.

"Saint Catherine."

"The wheel on which she died."

And so it went: twelve statues, twelve courageous stories, twelve forgotten Saints.

Toward the back, near the loading dock door, we came upon the altar bathed in the fading afternoon light streaming in through a dirty window. It was a regal affair, the sides and front swarming with meticulously carved and polished Angels. Already some other stuff had been set upon it—an electric fan, some soiled rags, and a stack of books.

Father approached the altar reverently, shoved the books to one side, and sadly placed his hands flat upon its surface. His eyes were riveted on something between them. Norman and I watched in questioning silence.

"Mr. Slater," said Father at last. "You're a Catholic."

"Not a good one, obviously," said the man. "I didn't know diddly about all those Saints back there."

"Nonetheless, you can appreciate this." Father stepped aside and pointed to a white rectangle of stone set in the center of the otherwise wooden surface. The stone was about ten inches by twelve. Five Crosses had been carved into its surface, four at the corners and one in the center.

"I don't get it," said Slater, examining the mysterious object.

"That's an altar stone," said Father. "Ring any bells?"

Suddenly the doors of Mr. Slater's soul opened wide. "You mean—?"

"Without a doubt," said Father, "there is a first class relic imbedded in that stone."

"You mean, a bit of ... a body?"

"A relic of a Saint."

"I thought they'd done away with that sort of thing," said Mr. Slater, "when they brought in the New Mass."

"Which is why this altar now stands in your warehouse," said Father. "Undoubtedly Father Upshaw has replaced it with a simple table."

"But what should I do about ... that stone?"

"That's up to you," said Father. "But be advised that relics cannot be bought and sold. No blessed object can. For a Catholic to do so is a sin."

"That's another thing they've done away with," commented the gardener. "Sin, I mean."

"You mean I've been swindled?" said Mr. Slater, jerking to attention. "Why that no good ... So what should I do?"

"I'd think long and hard about it," suggested Father. "If you returned this altar and the statues to Father Upshaw, he'd no doubt just sell them to someone else."

"Then I'm stuck with them."

"Well, like I said: think long and hard about it."

"You're not leaving."

"It's time that we pressed on."

Mr. Slater looked from Father to the altar stone, back to Father, then to the stone again. "Look Father, would you do me a favor? Could you maybe take the altar stone with you, at least, until I decide what to do about all these other things?"

"You're uneasy about relics?" asked Father.

"Let's just say that I haven't been around them much, and I'm the kind of guy who doesn't stroll through cemeteries at night."

Father nodded his understanding, though not his approval. He stepped back to the altar and gripped the edge of the stone with his fingertips. It lifted easily out of its recess, leaving a rectangular indentation in the wood about an inch deep.

"I will gladly take care of this for you until you reach your decision," said Father, turning to leave.

"Thank-you, Father. I owe you one."

"You owe it to yourself to give the matter serious consideration."

"That I will, Father. You can count on it."

9

"FATHER BAPTIST, YOU SAY," said the wobbly-jowled priest, motioning us into a sumptuous living room. He flopped himself into a marshmallow-shaped chair that hissed and squeaked as he slowly sank until his knees were level with his chins. "Have a seat, gentlemen. Have a seat."

"I'll stand, if you don't mind," I said, eyeing the puffy thing nearest me. "I don't think I'd ever be able to get up out of that again."

"Suit yourself," said Father Upshaw. "I could have someone bring in another chair."

"No need, Father," said Father Baptist, who also remained standing. "We won't take much of your time. Cardinal Fulbright has asked me to look into certain matters, and your name happened to come up when I was looking into them."

"Really," said Father Upshaw. "I'm afraid I don't understand."

"Mr. Goodman, the proprietor of a pawnshop on the next block, said that you sold him some sacred vessels."

"Oh those," said Father Upshaw, curling his lips into something resembling a summer squash. "Yes, they were just cluttering up the sacristy. We're into stoneware and crystal these days. Gold and silver are things of the past."

"I see," said Father. "Were you satisfied with the price Mr. Goodman paid you?"

"Can't say either way," shrugged the pastor. "I've no idea what they're worth. I just needed the space and he was handy."

"Could I ask what he did pay you?"

"I'd have to look it up. With all the remodeling and construction we've been doing here at Saint Lucy's, I've had more important matters on my mind."

"Did you perhaps make any attempt to distribute these items among your parishioners?"

"Never occurred to me. The cardinal's mandate is, 'Out with the old, in with the new.' Some of those things had been here since this church was built back in 1906."

"It never occurred to you that those things were purchased by the families who built this church with their hard-earned donations? Some of the older families might have jumped at the chance to have those sacred vessels in their possession."

Father Upshaw leaned forward, which was hard considering the position he was in. "I'm not sure I like your tone," he grunted, then settled back. "We're devoted to change here at Saint Lucy's. Our job is to build the future, not to pay lip service to the nostalgic urges of older folks."

"And the statues you sold to Mr. Slater," said Father, undaunted, "it never crossed your mind that some families with particular devotions to one Saint or another might like to have those works of art in their homes?"

"Such devotions, as you call them, are throwbacks to medieval thinking. Mere superstition. I'm not going to encourage such things."

"I see. And the high altar?"

"A block of wood. Too ornate. It was out of place in our refurbished church."

"Would you happen to have the authentication papers for the altar stone?"

"What altar stone?"

"The one that was still in the altar when you sold it."

"I have no idea." Father Upshaw looked flustered. "Now see here: I don't know what you're getting at or how these questions can possibly be part of whatever it is the cardinal wants you to do. I intend to call the Chancery in the morning and find out."

"You do that," said Father. "By the way, do you have a parishioner by the name of Archibald Roring?"

"Do I! He's been a thorn in my side for years. Talk about throwbacks. He wiggled his way onto the parish council and even the liturgical committee. He hates change, fights me at every turn. I wish he'd go join one of those illicit Tradition-alist chapels and leave me alone. Now is there anything else?"

"Not at present," said Father, turning toward the door. "But I'll probably be back."

10

"I'M SORRY, BUT I WAS JUST getting ready to leave for the night," said the man rising from behind his desk, slipping his arms into his jacket sleeves and straightening his tie. "If you'd like to make an appointment, I can fit you in Monday morning, say around ten."

"This will only take a minute," said Father, "and I think the subject is of some importance to you."

"Oh," said the man, suddenly focusing on Father's Roman collar. He snatched a pair of glasses from his blotter and slipped them onto his face. "I'm sorry, Father, I didn't real-ize. Do sit down."

"I'm Father John Baptist of Saint Philomena's parish. And this is my associate, Martin Feeney."

"I think I've heard about you," said the man. "You're a Traditionalist or something."

"You might say that."

"If you want to invest parish funds," said the man, "I've got something here that might interest you."

Something that was certainly of interest to me was a copy of the archdiocesan newspaper on the corner of the desk. It was folded inside out, and an article in the lower corner was circled in red ink: RELICS OF ST. VALERIA TO BE REMOVED FROM CATHEDRAL, said the heading. "TEMPORARY RELOCATION

DURING RENOVATION," SAYS CARDINAL. I thought to make a comment, but decided against it.

"It's not that," said Father. "You left your business card with Mr. Goodman at his pawnshop. You are Archibald Roring, are you not?"

"Why, yes."

"You made inquiries about certain sacred objects which Father Upshaw sold to him?"

"Indeed I did. The prices Mr. Goodman proposed were outrageous. Nonetheless, I'm in no position to argue. I'm trying to get a few friends to pool our resources so we can get those items back."

"Back?" asked Father.

"My father bought that monstrance as a gift to old Father McManigill when he was made a monsignor, back in '57. He died long before Upshaw took over. You bet I'd like it back."

"And you didn't know that Father Upshaw was going to sell the monstrance to Mr. Goodman?"

"No. I had suggested repeatedly to the parish council that we should construct a display case at the back of the church so those sacred objects wouldn't be entirely forgotten. Father Upshaw said he would consider it. He never let on that he was just going to sell those things outright. Why, it's sinful. It's an outrage."

"Yet you intend to buy them from the pawnshop?"

"If it's a matter of sin, Father, I'd say that buying those objects is a far lesser offense than standing by as they're purchased by people who don't have a clue as to their purpose, turning them into flower pots and such."

"You've got a point there. How close are you to your goal?"

"My friends and I will probably have the money together sometime next week. I've got five thousand of my own already, and they've promised to come up with the other fifteen. Why? Is there another buyer? I told Mr. Goodman to call me if there was."

"No, Mr. Roring, there is no other buyer. And there won't be."

"What do you mean?"

"Are you telling me that you are unaware that Mr. Goodman's shop was burglarized? That all those vessels and objects were taken, even the altar bells?"

"Good Heavens." Mr. Roring's jaw fell, pulling his eyebrows askew. "I didn't know."

"Are you telling me the truth, Mr. Roring?"

"How dare you suggest otherwise? Say, are you some kind of cop?"

"Used to be," said Father. "I'm a parish priest now, and it is in that capacity that I'm here. It's come to my attention that precious Catholic religious articles are being stolen all over the city. The police have even formed a task force to look into it. I strongly suggest that, if you are in any way involved, you tell me now—before the police get on your trail."

"My trail?"

"If I found you, the police will, too."

"But I haven't done anything wrong."

"But you've done something."

"What do you mean?"

Father drew close to Mr. Roring's desk. "I understand your distaste for the way Father Upshaw disposed of those treasures. I really do. I myself only say the Traditional Latin Mass at Saint Philomena's. If I had the money I'd go to every pawnshop in town and purchase every chalice and monstrance I could find and tuck them safely away for posterity. But I don't. Now, some people—people not unlike yourself—might decide that the lesser of two evils would be to steal those treasures rather than let them end up as flower pots."

"Desperate people do desperate things," said Mr. Roring. "And if there are people stealing sacred vessels for that reason, I applaud them. And if they get caught, I'd rally to their defense and raise money to pay their attorneys."

"Are you that desperate, Mr. Roring?" said a female voice from behind me.

I whirled to see Sybil Wexler standing there with Lieutenant Tragg Holcomb smiling at her side.

"Who are you?" said Mr. Roring, rising from his chair.

"Police," said Tragg, flashing his badge. "We'd like to ask you a few questions, Mr. Roring. And Baptist, we'd like you and your gardener to leave."

"Gardener?" said Roring, eyeing me.

"Associate gardener," I said as Father Baptist grabbed my arm and herded me past Sybil Wexler. "And if you ever visit Saint Philomena's, you can check my work."

I gave Officer Wexler a look of what I hoped was disappointment as I went by.

She didn't look happy. Nothing like her partner, anyway.

11

"JUST MADE IT!" I CRIED as I slid into my seat in the dining nook back at the rectory.

Father Baptist's billowing cassock was still deflating from his heroic leap into his chair from halfway across the kitchen. Monsignor Havermeyer, who had no doubt been sitting there for ten minutes, looked up from his evening paper, gave me a tired stare, and folded it up.

Millie's shadow stretched across the table, and suddenly a half-dozen bowls and plates landed thunderously in our midst. As usual, not a single crumb nor morsel ended up on the tablecloth.

"Grace," said Father.

We made the Sign of the Cross and bowed our heads. Millie's one-woman fight against silence was put on hold for the brief duration.

"Busy day, Father?" asked Monsignor Havermeyer at the conclusion.

"Very," said Father. "And how did confessions go?"

"I must say that the kinds of confessions I hear here are different from those I used to listen to at Saint Philip's."

"That's because," said the gardener, pouring dressing on his salad, "a different sort of folk attends Saint Philomena's."

GARDENING TIPS: At Saint Philip's confessions are heard in something called a "Reconciliation Booth." The penitent sits in a chair facing his confessor. Together they examine his progress in his "faith journey." They talk things out.

At Saint Philomena's we do it the old fashioned way: the penitent kneels in a small closet facing a veiled window behind which the priest sits, listens, assigns penances, and administers Absolution. No excuses asked for, no pretexts given, no rationalization allowed.

                                        --M.F.

N.B.: I've heard that at Saint Philip's the average penance is to "go and do something nice for someone." At Saint

Philomena's my sins and negligences gener-
ally get me the Stations of the Cross on
my knees. You wonder why I don't go to
Saint Philip's to get shriven? Well, I'm
one of those "different sort of folk" we
were just talking about.

Just then there was a knock at the door.

"I wonder who that could be," said Millie, stomping past
her sink and clutching the doorknob, the sinews of her fore-
arms gathering into ropy knots.

"No one," I whispered to Havermeyer. "No mortal man
may interrupt Millie's sacred meal times. I pity the poor fool
who's standing on the porch."

"Excuse me, Millie," said a voice as the door swung open.
"Hello, Father."

"Arthur?" said Father.

"Martin," said Arthur, gesturing with his finger, "could I
please speak with you a minute?"

"Why doesn't he just come in?" asked Monsignor Havermeyer.

"Once you enter the Millie Zone you have to stay and eat,"
I answered, clutching the edge of the table with one hand and
my cane with the other. Ah, l-l-l-l-leverage. Getting up is in-
evitably harder than sitting down. "Obviously Arthur is on
his way somewhere and doesn't want to get stuck here in the
land of shadow and substance, of things and ideas—"

"Martin," said Arthur again.

"You must stay, Monsignor, because you're a Monsignor,"
I explained, lumbering toward the door. "Whereas I, being
the help, can leave the Zone—"

"Hrmph," hrmphed Millie as I went by.

"—for a second or two, anyway," I concluded, lurching
outside. "What's the problem, Arthur? Hey, I like the new
vest. It goes well with your tailcoat."

"Thanks, Martin," he said, looking toward the front gate
and then back at me. "Sorry to disturb your dinner, but
we're on our way home from the airport, and Beth—that's my
sister—she would really like to meet you and Father Baptist."

"Well, bring her in," I said. "The worst thing that can
happen is she'll have to eat Millie's dinner, and it's far better
than what she got on the plane."

"No doubt," smiled Arthur. "But she's been having a lot
of spells on the way home."

"Narcolepsy, you called it this morning."

"Yes. It's a sleeping disorder. You know how sometimes you get tired—as in really tired—so sleepy that you sort of blank out for a second? Then you snap out of it and realize you just missed the last three words of what someone was saying? It's particularly dangerous when you're driving a car late at night."

"Or," I said, digging down into my bag of profundity, "having a late dinner with a hopeful girlfriend after you had to work past midnight the night before, and she's telling you the details of her shattered life."

"Right," laughed Arthur. "Well, Beth spends about half of her waking life asleep. She drifts off just like that, then wakes up a few minutes later. Then she's fine for a while, then she's out again. When she's stressed about something, the spells come quicker and shorter. I've seen her fall asleep and waken as fast as maybe once every eight seconds."

I whistled my astonishment. "I take it she can't drive."

"Or hold a normal job."

"That must pose quite a conundrum for you and your family."

"But nevertheless," he smiled, "she's my kid sister, and she's quite a gal once you get used to her nodding off on you. That's always been her problem with people: they get insulted over something she can't help. They think they're boring her."

"Does she sleep normally at night?"

"Yeah, pretty much. And sometimes she'll just pass out for an hour right in the middle of the day. There's no real pattern to it."

"And you're saying that her spells have been frequent since you left the airport? Are you sure you shouldn't just get her home and into bed?"

"No, she insisted. I've told her so much about you and Father Baptist, she just has to meet you now, tonight. She brought a wheelchair with her, but there's a lot of steps around here—"

"So you want Father to come out to the car," I surmised.

"Right."

"And that's why we're standing out here rather than back in the kitchen?"

"Isn't that what you explained to Monsignor Havermeyer?"

"Yes, but I wanted to hear how stupid it sounded coming from somebody else."

With that, I spun around—well, my awkward approximation thereof—and went back into the kitchen. "It would seem," I announced to all, "that Arthur's sister, Beth, is sitting out in the car. Her narcolepsy has been acting up during the drive from the airport, so Arthur told her to stay put and has requested that the mountains go to Mohammed."

"Narcolepsy?" asked Millie, setting down her skillet.

"A sleeping disorder," explained the smart gardener. " I think he's afraid that right now, while she's blacking out every few seconds, she could easily fall down or hurt herself some way."

"Then what are we waiting for?" roared Millie, untying her apron and tossing it on the rim of the sink. "Let's go meet the girl. I imagine we'll have to wade through a sea of those Tumblar fellows to get to her."

"No doubt," agreed Father, rising from the table. "Coming, Monsignor?"

"Of course," said Havermeyer, already on his feet.

We all followed Arthur through the garden, down the brick path, through the front gate, and down the cement steps to the curb. The Tumblars were, as predicted, in attendance. Joel and Jonathan were leaning against the side of Arthur's station wagon. Edward was busy rearranging something on the luggage rack—a collapsible wheelchair was visible amidst the suitcases.

Through the dirty side window we could see an attractive young woman seated—or rather slumped—in the back seat. She had long black hair, and her head was tilted in that manner peculiar to one who is fast asleep and enjoying it.

"Timing is everything," said Edward, finishing his business on the roof. He went around to the far side of the car, opened the door, and slipped in beside the sleeping beauty. "She seems to have lapsed again," he called through the glass.

"Oh, that's too bad," said Arthur. "I apologize, Father, Millie, Monsignor. When she gets like this, she may not wake up for an hour. I'm sorry I dragged you out here for nothing."

"Don't be silly," said Millie, bending over to get a good look at the sleeping girl. "My, Arthur, but she's pretty. She's got your nose."

"I'm glad she didn't get anything more of mine," said he.

"Come look at her, Father," said Millie, her nose almost against the window, waving her arm in insistent circles. "She's gorgeous, isn't she?"

"Indeed," said Father, stooping for a quick look.

"How long has she been like this?" asked Millie.

"Oh, since her late teens," said Arthur. "She was fine as a kid, but suddenly, during the last semester in high school, she started dozing off in class. The teachers weren't inclined to tolerate such behavior so they called Mom and Dad. She was diagnosed just after graduation, so her last grades in high school were very poor. Then her condition got rapidly worse. She never attended college, and she hasn't been able to hold down a job."

"How sad," said Millie, sniffing. "And so lovely. I doubt any man would want her."

"Not if he likes a wife who is attentive," said Edward.

"We're hoping," said Arthur, "that this Dr. Raphael Zaiden in Italy can help her. He's apparently had some success over there, but his methods haven't been approved by the AMA here in the States."

"I say, Arthur," said Jonathan, "this is all well and good, but don't you think we should take her to your place so she can stretch out on the couch or something?"

"You do that," said Millie. "And you boys treat her with kid gloves. Do you hear me?"

"Yes, M'am," they saluted together, then clambered to get in the car.

"I suggest we get back inside," said Father, "and finish our dinner."

"How sad," sniffed Millie, "how very, very sad."

12

"YOU FORGOT YOUR COFFEE," said Millie, slamming down the cup and saucer Monsignor had forgotten back in her domain. We were now in Father's study.

"Oh, sorry," said the monsignor, easing himself into my favorite chair's twin.

The gardener was already basking in his favorite chair and settling. He scooped up a book from an assortment piled next to him on the floor.

"Is that a detective novel?" asked Father, piling his pipe with aromatic tobacco.

"Craig Rice," I said, showing him the faded, tattered cover. "I found it in a used book store. *Trial by Fury.*"

"Wasn't Rice a woman?" asked Father.

"Her real name was Georgiana Ann Randolph Walker Craig Lipton DeMott Bishop," I read from the preface. "I can see how 'Craig Rice' saved a lot of ink as she wandered through life. One helluva writer, if you ask me."

"And since you yourself are a writer—" said Father.

"Trying to be," I corrected him.

"You're reading her for what?" asked Father. "Inspiration?"

"Starved for a plot?" asked Havermeyer, holding a cardboard match to his cigarette.

"Honing your detective skills?" asked Father, striking a wooden match against his shoe. "Studying the competition?"

"Actually, I'm just enjoying the read," I said, opening to a dog-eared page. "I love this John J. Malone character. He's got a peculiar wit: insightful, but with an underlying sarcasm. Here, listen to this:

> ... Everything, he decided, was almost unbearably sad. Life was wonderful, but nobody seemed to know what to do with it, and the world was beautiful, but nobody looked at it except tourists. He felt that he had discovered an important and impressive truth, and felt uncomfortably lonely about it. Here a kind of perfection of existence was always close at hand, and no one reached for it. Instead people hated each other, for inadequate reasons, small hotels were built without air-conditioning, and the damned birds woke one up at five in the morning.

"See what I mean?"

"I'd say he's got a depressing edge," said Father, expelling a mushroom of thick, blue smoke, "but the source of his melancholia is not the same as yours because your world view is so completely at variance with his. For that reason you couldn't write like that even if you wanted to."

"Come again?" asked Havermeyer, throwing his spent match into the wastebasket.

"I'm not sure that I could," said Father, rubbing his eyes. "It's been a long, long day."

Curling strands of smoke meandered around the small hand-carved statues of Saint Anthony of Padua and Saint Thomas More which stood guard on Father's desk.

"According to this bio at the back," I noted, "Rice converted to Catholicism toward the end of her life."

"Ave Maria," yawned Father. "Then we have good hope—"

Just then the front doorbell clanged.

"At this hour?" said Father wearily.

"I'll do the honors," I said, reaching for my cane.

"My turn," said Havermeyer.

"Oh bother," huffed Millie as she stomped by the doorway on her way down the hall. "I'll get it. I'm on my way out anyway. See ya!"

The sound of the latch, mumbled voices, the slam, approaching footsteps.

"Good evening, gentlemen," said Sybil Wexler. She was still wearing the red outfit, and it had been a long day for her, too. Her hair drooped somewhat and her jacket was disheveled. Her fulcra were wobbling with exhaustion.

Still, as a potential matrimonial prospect, she was well worth salvaging; and chivalry not being dead, I began the slow process of getting to my feet because a woman—true, the woman of my dreams, but nonetheless a woman—had just entered the room.

"Sorry to interrupt your male bonding session," said Tragg Holcomb, his dome no more bald, neither ear more drooped, his shoulders more stooped, nor his suit one seam more crooked than the first time I'd appraised his appearance that day.

GARDENING TIPS: He was changeless, in other words. But as you can see, if the crack about "male bonding" was the best he could do, he had no sense of humor whatsoever. Furthermore, I was coming to realize that he was one of those individuals who, the more they smile, the less they really mean it.

                                        —M.F.

"Well, you have," said Havermeyer, who made no pretense of chivalry or courtesy. He irritably exhaled a gush of smoke in Holcomb's general direction. "And at an inconvenient hour."

"The police," said Tragg, "have no inconvenient hours."

"Please," said Father who had risen to his feet, motioning Sybil toward the one remaining empty chair. It was the worst wreck in the study, but it was all that was left. Tragg, obviously, could remain standing.

"No thank-you," said Sybil. "Father Baptist, we need to ask you about the whatever-it-was you brought here after leaving—"

Willie's pouch! thought the gardener, falling back into his favorite chair. Luckily he couldn't verbalize this sentiment aloud because he had just swallowed his tongue.

"—Norman Slater's place of business this afternoon."

"Oh that," said Father, easing back into his chair behind the desk.

Oh that! sighed the gardener, relaxing. As he did so, the paperback dropped from his hand onto the pile of books on the floor.

"We'd really like to know what you took from the premises," said Tragg, smiling all the more, and so all the less.

"You will find seven sets of traditional liturgical vestments hanging in the closet in the sacristy," said Father.

"What is a sacristy?" asked Sybil.

"A room just off the Sanctuary in the church," said Father, "where I make preparations for saying Mass."

"Anything else?" asked Tragg.

"This," said Father, opening the drawer of his desk and indicating a rectangular object wrapped in a white cloth.

Tragg drew near and looked down into the drawer. "And what is that?"

"An altar stone," said Father. He made no move to take it out of the drawer. "Mr. Slater asked me to keep it for him while he made up his mind what to do with it."

"And why would he ask you to do that?" asked Tragg, turning his attention to a small plaque on the mantel above the fireplace near where I was sitting:

> I do not speak rashly, but as I feel and think. I do not think that many priests are saved, but that those who perish are far more numerous. The reason is that the office requires a great soul. For there are many things to make a priest swerve from rectitude, and he requires great vigilance on every side.
> —St. John Chrysostom

Tragg's smile faded as he pondered the words, then regrouped as he turned back to Father. "Where was I? Oh yes. Why did Mr. Slater ask you to keep this ... er ... artifact?" "You'd have to ask Mr. Slater," said Father. "I'd prefer that he tell you."

"No doubt you would," said Tragg, stealing a final glance at the plaque and filing it away in his brain which, no doubt, boasted the same clay-like appearance as his face. "But as we're already here, perhaps you could enlighten us."

"An altar stone is a particularly precious thing," explained Father. "It is a holy object—something which cannot be licitly bought or sold. It contains the relics of a Saint, usually a Martyr."

"Ah," smiled Tragg. "I see we're talking 'relics' again."

"And I'll be glad to keep right on talking about them," said Father, "all night, if you wish—well, perhaps not all night, but for a fair amount of time at any rate—but only if you two explain why this is any concern of yours."

"Norman's Studio Supply was burglarized," said Sybil, "less than an hour ago."

"Indeed," said Father, eyebrows raised. He blew a perfect smoke ring that hovered between Saint Anthony and Saint Thomas More. "Tell us more."

"Someone apparently rammed a large truck into the back door of the warehouse," said Sybil. "Mr. Slater says they took a wooden altar and twelve large statues. Does that mean anything to you?"

"We saw them there," said Father. "I understand that they were sold to Mr. Slater by Father Upshaw, pastor of Saint Lucy's. But surely Mr. Slater told you that."

"Well, there we have a problem," said Tragg. "Mr. Slater was apparently working late and was standing near the back door when it was rammed. When the door imploded, he was knocked pretty hard. He managed to talk to the first officer on the scene, but then he lapsed into unconsciousness. He's at Good Samaritan Hospital, unable as yet to answer questions."

"That is deplorable," said Father.

"What is also deplorable," said Tragg, "not to mention intriguing, is the fact that religious objects seem to vanish after inquiries have been made about them."

"You're referring to Mr. Goodman's pawnshop," said Father, "and Archibald Roring."

"And others," said Tragg. "It would almost seem—"

Just then the phone on the desk rang.

"Excuse me," said Father, snatching up the receiver. "Saint Philomena's Rectory. Yes? Duggo? Where are you calling from? What's wrong?" We could hear little chipmunk noises emanating from the earpiece—a chipmunk with a Spanish accent. "And he's gone to investigate? You haven't heard from him? I think you'd better ... Yes, I'll hold on."

Father looked at me during the silence.

"Trouble at the mausoleum," he said. Then the receiver exploded with excitement. "Slow down, Duggo. Give it to me slow and easy ... Okay, okay. Notify the police. Martin and I will be right over."

He set the receiver in its cradle.

"What's wrong?" asked Sybil.

"Yes," smiled Tragg. "Do tell us."

"Roberto and Duggo occasionally moonlight at New Golgotha," said Father, knocking the smoldering ashes out of his pipe into an ashtray. "A third guard, Galloway I think he said, was just making his rounds in the mausoleum, keeping in touch with Roberto and Duggo in the guardhouse via walkietalkie. Galloway reported something amiss in the crypt where Saint Valeria is now interred. Galloway's report was suddenly cut off. Roberto went to investigate. That's when Duggo called."

"And why should he call you?" asked Tragg.

"Because I'm an interested party," said Father. "Martin and I were there this afternoon."

"You do get around," remarked Tragg.

"And then what happened," asked Havermeyer, "to cause all the excitement?"

"Roberto just called Duggo on the walkie-talkie," said Father. "He thinks Galloway is dead. You heard me tell him to notify the police." He got up from his chair. "Martin, we have to leave immediately."

"Not so fast," said Tragg. "We're not finished—"

Something chirped in Sybil Wexler's red purse. She reached inside, retrieved a cell phone, flipped it open, then held the device against the side of her face.

"Wexler," she said. A little voice warbled in her ear. "Got it. We're on our way."

"What's up?" asked Tragg as she shoved the phone back into her purse.

"They want us to get over to New Golgotha," said Sybil.
"Something's been stolen."

"From a cemetery?" asked Tragg. "What now?"

"I'll fill you in on the way," she said.

"So," said Father, "it would seem that our paths are about
to run parallel courses this evening."

"See that they don't intersect," said Tragg.

The phone on the desk rang again.

Father was just in the process of donning his overcoat, so I
grabbed it. "Saint Philomena's," I said sweetly.

Willie Kapp's voice jabbered excitedly in my ear. I could
hear his dreadlocks rattling for emphasis.

"Willie ask, an' Father Jack come," he was saying. "Willie
ask for trust, an' Father give trust. Now Willie ask dah t'ird
favor, dah most dah hon'rable mon can ask dah fren in one
day."

"Father Baptist is right here," I said, trying to sound reas-
suring. "What do you need?"

"Come, right away."

"Who is it?" asked Father.

"You'd better take it," I said, handing him the phone.

"Yes?" said Father into the receiver.

Willie rattled his dreadlocks in Father's ear while I grunted
and groaned my way to a standing position.

"Are you in danger?" asked Father. "You're sure? Okay,
listen: I can't come immediately. I'm with the police and we
need to take care of something first."

"If it's something I can handle—" offered Havermeyer.

Father shook his head at the monsignor, then turned his attention back to the phone. "I will get there just as soon as I
can. That's the best I can do. Lock the doors and wait for
me."

Willie rattled something further as I took my cane from its
place next to the fireplace.

"Okay, sit tight," said Father, hanging up the phone.

"Problem?" asked Tragg.

"One of my flock in trouble," said Father.

"You're sure I can't be of help?" asked Havermeyer.

"Not at present," said Father. "But I suspect an already
long day is going to stretch itself into a longer night. Do you
think you're ready to say Mass?"

"You mean tomorrow?" asked Havermeyer skeptically.

GARDENING TIPS: Monsignor Havermeyer, who
had only joined us a couple of months before, had been practicing the rubrics of
the Old Rite every night in his top-heavy
R.V. which occupied two of the five spaces
in the back parking lot. He also lived
back there, preferring his camper to a
cozy room in the rectory under Millie's
watchful skillet.

                                        --M.F.

"Well?" asked Father.

"I'm sure I'll never be ready," said Havermeyer, "but I'll
give it my best shot, if you need me to."

"I do," said Father. "I may be back by then, but probably
without any sleep."

"Very well," sighed Havermeyer, getting up from his chair.
"If you need me, I'll be reviewing my missal all night."

"Thank-you," said Father. "Martin, let's go."

Sybil Wexler, all red and weary, and her sidekick Tragg, all
clay and smiles, were already gone.

13

"I'M SO GLAD THAT YOU are here, Father," said Duggo,
clutching Father's hand.

"Galloway," said Roberto, somewhat dazed, "he is dead."

Duggo and Roberto crossed themselves.

"So I understand," said Father, doing likewise.

"And Saint Valeria," said Roberto, as if in a dream, "... she
is ... she is..."

Roberto, Duggo, Father, and I were standing in an arched
room just off the crypt in the mausoleum. Policemen and lab
technicians were milling all around. Through the archway
and amidst many moving officers I could see the form of a
man in a security guard's uniform on the floor, face down, his
head inches from the resting-place of Saint Valeria. The
blank facing stone was no longer cemented in place. It had
been removed, revealing a black, empty rectangular hole in
the lower wall. Yes, I said empty. The coffin containing Saint
Valeria was *gone,* and the facing stone itself was on the floor,

propped against the dead guard's head. The guard's hair was matted with blood, and a dark stain was pooling on the floor. It was not a pretty sight.

"Who would steal a Saint's body?" asked Duggo.

"And kill a guard in the process?" added the gardener.

"Good question," said a familiar voice.

"Lieutenant Taper," said Father, turning.

"Jack," acknowledged Taper. "What brings you here?"

"Duggo called me at the rectory from the guardhouse," said Father.

"Sí," said Duggo. "It's like I just told you—"

"Yes, yes," said Sergeant Wickes, Taper's partner, emerging from the crypt. "We know what you said. Galloway was making a report on the walkie-talkie when something caught his eye in the crypt."

"Sí, Señor Wickes," said Duggo. "He say something flashed in the beam of his flashlight. He say he was checking it out."

"Flashed?"

"That is what he say."

"Then we hear a noise," said Roberto. "A loud noise."

"Over the walkie-talkie?" asked Taper.

"Sí," said Roberto and Duggo together.

"Then silence?" asked Taper.

"Just the static," said Duggo.

"And you went to see what was wrong," said Taper. "You were armed?"

"Sí," said Roberto, his hand moving automatically to the holster on his belt. Then he pointed to the form on the floor, "And I find him just like this."

"And you saw no one else?" asked Wickes.

"No one," said Roberto emphatically. "You think I would not tell you if I did?"

"It depends who you saw," said Wickes. "And what were you doing at the time, Duggo?"

"I was speaking on the phone with Father Baptist," said Duggo, "when Roberto call in."

"And?" asked Taper.

"And Father tell me to call you."

"Very civic-minded of him," said another voice. Tragg emerged from the next room, rubbing dust from his hands. "I still think it strange that you should have called him rather than the police in the first place."

"I did not know yet what was wrong," said Duggo. "But I knew that Father, he would be interested."

"I'll bet," said Tragg.

"And what's your interest in this?" asked Taper, turning to Tragg.

"Officer Wexler and I are on a task force," said Tragg, "assigned to investigate the theft of religious objects. The body of this Saint Valeria would seem to fall into that category."

"And you think," said Father, "that the perpetrator was interrupted in his work by Galloway and killed him."

"That would seem to follow," smiled Tragg.

"It's a logical deduction," added Wickes.

"But you're not dealing with a single perpetrator here," said Father.

"How so?" asked Taper.

"It took six of us to carry that coffin into the mausoleum from the hearse," said Father.

"Six men?" said Tragg skeptically. "To carry one young woman—or should I say, what little was left of her? Come, come. She's been dead for centuries. Surely a few bones—"

"The coffin," said Father, "was made long ago in Europe from solid oak and overlaid with lead. It was heavy, I assure you."

"I don't suppose you looked inside," said Tragg, his smile deflating.

"The coffin was sealed with lead solder," said Father.

"I see," said Tragg, his smile gradually returning. "So as far as you know, there wasn't anything in the coffin in the first place."

Father gave Tragg a look that seemed to say, exhausted yet disgustedly, "Considering that you are suspicious of everything I say, and since I know the ground upon which I stand, you will draw your own conclusions—and they'll no doubt be wrong." Exhaling slowly, he simply turned away.

Just then Sybil emerged from the crypt.

"Find anything?" asked Tragg.

"They're dusting for prints," she said. "The floor hasn't been swept for some time, and there are a lot of scuffs and footprints in the dust. But with all the activity earlier today, the evidence is pretty confused."

"Duggo," said Father, "you said that Galloway reported something that caught his attention in the beam of his flashlight. He didn't say what it was?"

"No, Father. He say he was going to check it out—"

"Excuse me," intruded another voice. A husky uniformed police officer came stomping into the room from the direction of the front entrance. "Lieutenant Taper, we just caught someone on the grounds. He's acting very strange. Says his name is Archibald Roring, and his driver's license checks out. No priors."

"Mr. Roring," mused Tragg. "Now that *is* interesting."

"He had a newspaper on his desk when we talked with him in his office this afternoon," said Sybil. "He had circled an article about Saint Valeria being moved here today."

"And now he's found prowling around the grounds," said Tragg.

"Is that what he was doing?" asked Father to the officer who had brought the news. "Prowling?"

"Not exactly," said the cop. "We found him sprawled on the grass between a couple of large headstones about a hundred yards from the mausoleum. He smelled of liquor, and seemed to be just coming to. When we asked him what he was doing, he said he was hiding."

"Did you ask him who he was hiding from?" asked Taper.

"Yes," said the officer. "He said we wouldn't believe him."

"I think I want to talk to Mr. Roring," said Taper.

"You do that," said Father. "Martin and I must be going. I'd like to know what you find out. Would you care to drop by the rectory tomorrow morning after Mass?"

"That I will," said Taper.

"And what makes you two so cozy?" asked Tragg.

"Father Baptist," said Taper, "was once my superior officer. Didn't you know? He was Jack Lombard, Chief of Homicide."

"Really," said Tragg as if he didn't already know, the corners of his smile almost meeting behind his neck. "That is *most* interesting."

14

"UH OH," I SAID AS I BRAKED THE JEEP to a halt in front of Willie's shop.

"'Uh oh' is right," said Father, eyeing the front door.

The boulevard was very dark. The nearest working street lamp was halfway down the block. Still, we could see that the door was wide open.

"Hurry," said Father, leaping from the car.

He was already inside by the time I had disengaged my aching body from the driver's seat and traversed the sidewalk. I paused to catch my breath at the entrance, noticing as I did so that the wooden doorframe was splintered. The tongue of the deadbolt was still extended. Apparently the door had been kicked in with considerable violence—that, or the wooden frame was so rotten that a child could have done it. It was hard to tell without more careful examination, and it was far too dark for that without a flashlight.

"Father?" I said into the gloom beyond the doorway.

"Over here," called Father. "See if you can find the light switch."

I groped around the inside wall until I touched something, or it touched me. It wasn't a light switch. I pulled back my hand.

"Hurry with that light," snapped Father.

Tentatively, I groped around with my hand again. I found the switch and flipped it.

Yellow light from three bare bulbs hanging from the ceiling filled the room. Everything in the glass cases wiggled at once, then settled down again as I hobbled in the direction of Father's voice.

I found him behind one of the counters, kneeling beside the form of Guillame du Crane Cristal, also known as Willie Kapps. Willie's head was propped against Father's thigh.

"Willie," said Father. "Willie! Can you hear me?"

The victim's eyes fluttered open, spun around a few times, and then found their way toward Father Baptist's face. "Ah ... hear ya ... Jack."

"What happened?" whispered Father. "Can you tell me?"

"Knock at door," mumbled Willie. "Voices ... threats ... bangin' ... den 'Boom!' ... inside ... grabbed Willie ... wanted dah old t'ings ..."

"What's that?" hissed Father. "What old things?"

"Really old t'ings," said Willie. "Really old ... den dey ... oooh, my head."

"Martin," said Father, "call an ambulance. Then call the police."

"My trust," coughed Willie. "It ... safe?"

"Your trust is safe with me," said Father. "You can count on it."

"Need ... nuthah ... favor," rasped Willie as I dashed around—well, my approximation thereof—looking for the phone.

"I thought you told Martin," said Father, "that three favors were the most you could ask in one day."

"Oh," said Willie. "Is it midnight, yet?"

"No," said Father, glancing at his watch. "Ten 'til."

"Hmmm," said Willie, sinking. "So ... sue ... me ..."

I finally found the phone next to the cash register. I punched 911.

"... sue me," mumbled Willie. "... sue ..."

Sunday, November Twelfth

**Feast Day of Saint Pope Martin,
defender of the Faith against the Monothelites,
sentenced to die of starvation
on the island of Chersonese (655 AD)**

Another Namesake's Feast Day!!

∞ **Twenty-second Sunday after Pentecost** ∞

15

"HOC EST ENIM CORPUS MEUM," whispered Monsignor Havermeyer. He was standing at the altar, leaning forward, his lips inches from the large white host gripped in his trembling fingers.

For this is My Body.

"My Lord and my God," whispered the gardener as Joey, the altar boy, rang the bells.

Monsignor Havermeyer, dressed in regal vestments —courtesy of Norman Slater—genuflected, then raised the Transubstantiated Host above his head. The bells rang again. Another altar boy, Gordy, rocked the censer in earnest, sending plumes of fragrant smoke ceiling-ward. The monsignor set the Host down reverently and genuflected again. Joey responded with another round of rings.

It was Sunday Mass. Father Baptist, attired in cassock and surplice, was kneeling off to the left in the sanctuary beneath the statue of the Blessed Virgin. His face was buried in his weary hands.

Yours truly, similarly attired, was kneeling at the opposite side from Father, an old Latin-English missal open on the

floor before me. In spite of the importance of the moment, I
was expending most of my resources trying not to fall asleep.

"Simili modo postwuam cœnatam est," whispered Monsignor Havermeyer, turning his attention to the Chalice before
him, "accipiens et hunc præclarum Calicem in sanctas ac ven-
erabiles manus suas ..."

*In like manner, after He had supped, taking also this excel-
lent Chalice into His holy and venerable hands ...*

Monsignor Havermeyer was doing remarkably well. Except
for a few understandable mix-ups during the Offertory, he
looked and sounded—at least from the perspective of the
congregation who could only see his back—like a seasoned
veteran.

> GARDENING TIPS: Of course, from where I
> was kneeling, I could see the already-
> warped skin of his forehead contorting
> even further, so intense was the monsi-
> gnor's concentration. Still, all those
> nights of irritating rehearsal in the
> R.V.--often egged on by the undaunted
> pokes and prods of the parish gardener--
> were finally paying off.
>
> > --M.F.

> N.B. Yes: it had been worth it.

Thirty minutes later, his first Latin Mass concluded, Monsignor Havermeyer processed behind the string of altar boys
into the sacristy.

"O clemens," sang the choir as Father and I followed, " O
pia, O dulcis Virgo Maria."

O clement, O loving, O sweet Virgin Mary.

I noticed, just as I exited, that the Tumblars were seated in
the front row. Joel, Jonathan, Pierre, Arthur and Edward were
all attired in suits and ties. In their midst, between Arthur and
Pierre, sat Beth. Poor thing, she had slept right through Mass,
and was even now sinking down in the pew. Arthur kept
propping her up, and she kept slipping down again. Her head
fell forward and her long black hair spilled down over her
knees. When her brother righted her, her hair flowed the
other way over the back of the pew. It would have been comi-
cal if her condition wasn't so disruptive to any kind of a nor-

mal life—and certainly not conducive to concentrating during Mass.

Poor, poor woman, I thought as I exited the sanctuary. What's Arthur going to do when his parents get too told to take care of her?

A moment later I found the monsignor in the sacristy leaning against the counter, too emotionally and mentally exhausted to begin the process of removing his vestments. The altar boys were scurrying around, putting things away so they could run outside and enjoy the sunshine. The lads seemed to take particular delight in playing tag amidst the headstones in the cemetery behind the church.

"Monsignor," I said as I approached, shifting my cane to my left hand so that I could extend my right.

"Don't say it, Feeney," he growled. "I know I botched the Offertory."

"You did?" I asked innocently. "Good Heavens, I didn't notice. What'd you do?"

"Either you're lying or you were asleep," said Havermeyer.

"I always lie when I'm asleep," I winked, "which is why it's a good thing I never married."

"Hrmph," he hrmphed.

"Considering the circumstances," said Father Baptist, rubbing the flakes from his eyes—he hadn't had a wink of sleep all night, "you are to be congratulated, Monsignor. Your first Latin Mass went far better than my own."

"Sure, sure," sighed Havermeyer, finally starting to remove his vestments.

"Indeed," said Father. "In my case, I got the water and wine mixed up and had to redo the Offertory. I read the wrong Preface. Then I skipped a page during the remembrances. I was so mixed up I think I gave the final blessing after the Last Gospel instead of before. Fortunately, I said it in private. I'm lucky that God the Father, 'who seeth in secret,' didn't strike me with lightning."

"Saint Matthew six six," nodded the gardener, "and, um, Saint Luke seventeen twenty-four—sort of, kind of."

"You're not a good liar either, Father," said Havermeyer, "but I'm grateful for the attempt."

"There are liars, and there are liars," said a voice from the side door.

"Larry," said Father, walking over and shaking Lieutenant Taper's hand. "I'm glad you came."

"Are you going to make your usual after-Mass rounds among your parishioners?" asked Taper. "You know, the curious local tradition where the flock gets to sheer the shepherd?"

"Not today," said Father, shaking the sleep from his eyes. "I'm all spent. You'll do the honors, Monsignor?"

"Sure," said Havermeyer, removing his stole. "Why not? This seems to be my day."

"I think you'll find our parishioners impressed and appreciative," I said as I followed Father and Lieutenant Taper out the side door. I paused for a long moment on the threshold, arranging my face into an expression that I hoped conveyed sincerity. It took an effort. "And that, Monsignor, is no lie."

It's about seventy-five feet from the sacristy door on the side of the church to the kitchen door. Father Baptist and Lieutenant Taper had already crossed it and achieved the safety of the rectory. A few parishioners were milling around as I lurched and hobbled past them, hoping to make it to the rectory without being drawn into their meandering Sunday controversies. This was not my day.

"There's Mr. Feeney," I heard Mrs. Theodora Turpin say to her husband, Tanner.

"Yes, Dear," agreed her husband as they approached. "It most assuredly is."

"And he looks like he's in a hurry."

"Indeed he does, Dear."

"But he won't mind if I ask him."

"Decidedly not, Dear."

"Oh Mr. Feeeeeeeeeney!"

"Good morning, Mr. and Mrs. Turpin," I said, reluctantly slowing to a halt. "And how are you today?"

"We were wondering why Father Baptist didn't say Mass," said Mrs. Turpin. She elbowed her husband, Tanner. "Weren't we?"

"Oh yes, Dear."

"Monsignor Havermeyer felt that he was ready," I explained, "and since Father Baptist was not feeling quite himself this morning —"

"Mistah Feeney, Mistah Feeney," intruded another voice.

"Ah," I said, smiling as best I could, "Mrs. Cladusky."

"Muriel," said the squat woman who came waddling toward me. "When will ya and Faddah remembah to call me Muriel?"

"I wonder," I heard Mrs. Turpin saying off to the side, "who Father Baptist was feeling like this morning?"

"I can't imagine, Dear," said Tanner.

"I saw Faddah up in front," Mrs. Cladusky, who had filled my range of vision by this time, was saying, "but now he's gone."

"He's indisposed, I'm afraid," I said, looking apologetic. "He's been working on—"

"Well, ya tell him," said Mrs. Cladusky, "that my Bennie's come home from the cure. Ya tell him that, will ya? We'll have Faddah ovah fah dinnah some day soon."

"I'm sure he'll be pleased on both counts," I assured her.

"Millie came ovah last night, chuh know."

"So I understand. How was 'Religion Revisited'?"

"Awful, simply awful.."

"I've heard it's not worth seeing."

"Ya heard right."

"Who would watch such a thing?"

She looked at me long and hard as though peering at an *Imbecilicus ignoramus* in a cage at the zoo. "Me, Bennie, and Millie—or wasn't ya listening?"

Out of the corner of my eye I saw the Tumblars emerging from the side door of the nave. Arthur was slowly and carefully pushing Beth in her wheelchair, but even so it was a bumpy ride on the brick walkway. Her long hair swung this way and that as her head lolled in deep slumber. Parishioners made way for the curious procession that veered away from where I stood and headed toward the front gate.

"Oh," Mrs. Cladusky squeaked, remembering something. "Did ya know that my good friend, Mrs. Magillicuddy, is back from visiting huh sistah in Hemmet?"

"Yes, I know. She came by to let us know Friday evening."

"It's so good to have huh home, safe and sound. It's like I was just telling Bennie last night ovah dinnah—"

"You are stark raving mad," snarled Mrs. Patricia Earheart, jabbing her finger at Mr. Gregory Holman as they sauntered through, right between Mrs. Cladusky and myself. "How can you say such a thing?"

"Because it's true," said Holman, shoving her finger aside.

"It's can't be—Good morning, Mr. Feeney."

"But it is—Hi, Martin."

"Hello," I said as they passed, and "Good-bye," as I headed for the door once again.

"Where is he?" I heard a gruff voice behind the gathering cluster of heads.

I'd know Thurgood T. Turnbuckle's growl anywhere, and I was in no mood to deal with him just then. All bets off, I lunged for the kitchen. Once inside, I leaned back against the door, panting.

Millie's domain was eerily quiet, perhaps because Millie was outside somewhere, mingling with the masses. I might've stayed to savor the moment, but I was curious to know what Lieutenant Taper and Father Baptist were discussing.

I found them in the study. Father was trying to summon enough concentration to fill his pipe, but with questionable success.

"I understand that Willie Kapps got nailed last night," Taper was saying. "That you and Martin found him injured in his store after you left the cemetery."

"Are we being followed?" asked Father, setting the pipe down on the blotter. It wobbled and finally fell over on its side, spilling a few fronds of dark tobacco onto the ink-stained surface.

"Who would be tailing you?" asked Taper.

"Wexler and Holcomb," said Father.

"I wouldn't know about that," said Taper. "I heard about your visit to Willie's when I was at the hospital. After all, that's where the whole party finally migrated sometime this morning."

"Willie ended up in room 304," I said, groping my way to my favorite chair. "Norman Slater was in 305 right across the hall."

"When we left the hospital," said Father, "Willie had lapsed into unconsciousness, and Mr. Slater was still that way. How about Roring?"

"He's in the basement," said Taper. "Room 55B."

"The psycho ward?" asked the gardener, descending into his chair.

"Just for observation," said Taper. "And it's the neuro-psychiatric floor. He was pretty upset."

"What about?" asked Father.

"First he said we wouldn't believe him. Then he started talking about ghosts, then vampires. Something about the dead rising from the grave—"

"Not again!" winced the gardener.

"Martin," said Father, rubbing his eyes, "as you walked from the church to the rectory a few moments ago, did you happen to look up at the sky?"

"Yes, Father, that is, when I wasn't avoiding Mr. Turnbuckle."

"Any unusual cloud cover, weather patterns, that sort of thing?"

"Not that I noticed."

"Then I think we can rule out vampires," said Father, turning his tattered attention back to Lieutenant Taper. "What was that you were saying about Archibald Roring?"

GARDENING TIPS: Father was referring to the "Vampire's Shroud," a meteorological phenomenon which has been known to accompany the presence of the vurkolak. Really. Father had just had a run-in with one of them the previous Halloween — again, really. Yes, I had only just started pecking away at it in the wee hours on Dad's old Underwood, so it was far from done, and even farther from publication. I had a pretty good title figured out though: The Darkness Did Not.

—M.F.

"Like I said," resumed Taper, "he ranted for a while about ghouls and vampires. Then he settled down into meaningless monosyllables. The doc gave him something to make him sleep—says he won't come around 'til sometime this afternoon."

"Any idea when he went to the cemetery?" asked Father.

"Well," said Taper, "as far as we can reconstruct things, Sybil and Tragg kept him at his office until shortly after six. He did say something about having dinner at a restaurant. Darby's—we've checked on that."

"The man has good taste," noted the gardener.

"The hostess remembers him," said Taper, ignoring me, "and says he left sometime between seven and seven-thirty, but she's not certain. She remembered him because he had been drinking so heavily the bartender put a lid on his tab."

"Hm," said Father, shaking his head again. "That might explain his confusion about later events. I suspect that Tragg grilled him pretty hard in his office after showing us the door."

"I'd be tempted to down a few after a go-round with him," said the gardener helpfully. "Not that I actually would, of course, but—"

"And Norman Slater's place," said Father, ignoring me, "was invaded around eight?"

"That's right," said Taper.

"Wexler and Holcomb barged in here around nine," said Father. "They said the burglary at Norman's had taken place an hour before. Then Duggo called shortly thereafter, and Willie minutes after that."

"And in between," I interjected, "Sybil received a call on her cell phone, telling her to get over to the cemetery right away. The police sure acted fast."

"Sometimes we do," said Taper. "The minute Duggo's call came in and he mentioned Saint Valeria—not that her body had been stolen, but that the murder had been committed at her crypt—Chief Billowack notified Burglary, and they called Sybil within seconds. Everyone downtown is aware of the string of thefts, and of Cardinal Fulbright's interest, and the old Bulldog played a hunch that another theft might be involved."

"A rare moment of insight on his part," said Father. "Good for him."

"I don't think he or anyone yet realized the body had been stolen," said Taper. "I still don't figure it. It's one thing to steal a chalice or a reliquary, but a whole body—"

"Along with a lead coffin," added yours truly.

"It would require manpower," said Father, "not to mention a truck. Neither Galloway, Roberto, nor Duggo mentioned anything about seeing a truck on the premises."

"True," said Taper, "but after all, it's a big cemetery—I forget how many acres—with roads that wander all over the place. And it's hilly. There are lots of places you could park a truck that the guards wouldn't notice unless they were walking the grounds and came upon it."

"Don't they?" asked Father. "Walk the grounds?"

"Normally," said Taper, "once every hour and a half. But two of the regular guards called in sick, and Roberto and Duggo were just pinch-hitting. I guess they didn't follow the usual routine."

"Hmm," said Father, catching himself from drifting off to sleep. "Something odd about that."

"You think so?" asked Taper.

"I'd hardly call what's going on in my head 'thinking,'" said Father, rubbing his swollen eyes.

"Jack," said Taper, "you were talking about times a moment ago. Were you getting at something?"

"Hm?" asked Father sleepily. "Oh, not really ... I'm was just trying to get the sequence of events straight in my head ... A lot went on last night ... a lot ... went on ..."

Taper looked at me.

I looked at Taper.

"I think he's asleep," I whispered.

"I think I'll leave," said Taper.

"Do that," I said. "I think I'll just sit here and think a while."

16

"HI MARTIN," SAID LIEUTENANT TAPER into my ear. I had just answered the phone, you see. "Is Father Baptist awake yet? I need to talk to him."

"Lieutenant Taper wants to know if you're awake yet," I said, handing the phone across the desk. "You want to tell him, or shall I?"

"Hi, Larry," said Father, ignoring me. "What's up?"

Father Baptist had actually slept right through the afternoon. When Millie roused him at dinnertime, he had acknowledged her summons but somehow got sidetracked en route to the kitchen and wound up face down on that hard slab he calls a bed in his private quarters. Even Millie wasn't about to overlay her culinary demands on Father when he's that darn tired.

She left a casserole in the fridge for him to reheat in the oven when he got hungry, and withdrew to her own room.

GARDENING TIPS: Yes, "reheat" is what I said. We have no microwave at Saint Philomena's. For that matter, we don't have a dishwasher, food processor, stereo, television, or even an answering machine. Millie does have a washer and dryer for doing the clothes--and Mr. Folkstone is

```
always threatening to fix them so they'll
work for a change.  Ah, life in L.A ...!
                                   --M.F.
```

Sometime after dark I found Father eating Millie's gift in the dining nook; and finally, two rounds of coffee later, we found ourselves seated in the study. I had just finished reading *Trial by Fury* by Craig Rice—or whatever her name was—and was pondering the relative advantages of *The Case of the Hesitant Hostess* by Erle Stanley Gardner versus *Even in the Best of Families* by Rex Stout when Lieutenant Taper phoned. Of course, there was always the *Breviloquium* by Saint Bonnaventure or *A Dialogue of Comfort against Tribulation* by Saint Thomas More, but I just wasn't in the mood.

"Thank-you for telling me, Larry," Father was saying. "You can count on my discretion." He cradled the receiver.

"What was that all about?" I asked, dropping my books on the floor and stretching back in my chair.

"Larry shouldn't be sticking his neck out," said Father, rubbing the back of his own, "passing on police information to me like that. But I do appreciate it."

"So what's up?"

"It seems that just about the time we were visiting Archibald Roring in his office, with Wexler and Holcomb about to barge in, Dennis Goodman received a large bulging envelope in the afternoon post. It contained $20,500 in cash."

"Cash? Was it registered?"

"No, and no return address. It was postmarked the previous day in Van Nuys."

"That's not much to go on."

"It's certainly a risky way to deliver money. Two hundred and five one-hundred dollar bills. Dennis notified the police, and Burglary sent someone to fetch it. They found no fingerprints, but they recorded the serial numbers on the bills. They're holding on to it, much to Mr. Goodman's dismay."

"So much for good citizenship."

"Larry said he was only passing on office chatter, but from what he heard the numbers on those bills weren't consecutive. If they had been they probably could have been traced to a commercial banking or Federal Treasury source, but as it is they were just a hodgepodge of old currency. I don't think that's going to help the police much."

"Hmm," I said, looking at the ceiling. "Didn't Roring say that he had five thousand dollars ready to pitch into the pool his friends were getting together to pay for the objects in Mr. Goodman's shop?"

"Yes."

"And weren't his friends going to put together another fifteen thousand? That makes twenty thousand dollars."

"Too close to be a coincidence, I think," said Father.

"But what about that extra five hundred?"

"I don't know."

"Anything else?"

"Just that Archibald Roring came out of his drug-induced sleep around three this afternoon."

"And?"

"Now he's confused, withdrawn, and unwilling to talk about whatever it was he saw or did last night. Larry proposed that I visit Mr. Roring in the hospital tomorrow morning. I'm glad he made the suggestion because it would be more difficult for me to ask."

"Good," I said. "Anything else?"

Just then we heard a sound.

"Could that be someone knocking at the front door?" I said, grunting to my feet.

"I'll come with you," said Father. "You never know. It's after ten."

We found Edward on the front porch.

"I didn't want to knock loud enough to wake Millie," he explained. "I saw your light in the study. I was going to tap at the window next."

"Oh great," I said, "with officers from Burglary dropping by at all hours, all we need is for them to find you slinking around the rectory in the dark."

"I guess you might say they already found us," he said, hooking his thumb over his shoulder.

Arthur's station wagon was parked in front of the rectory. A police car had pulled in behind it, all crooked so its rear end stuck out into the street. Police do that sometimes, I think, just because they can get away with it. The Tumblars were gathered on the sidewalk, chatting amongst themselves—except for Arthur, who was explaining the sleeping woman in the back seat to Sybil Wexler, and Pierre, who was engaged in a lively discussion with none other than Lieutenant Tragg Holcomb.

"That's just terrible," Sybil was saying. "You mean she just drops off any time?"

"Usually it's rapid spurts," said Arthur. "But sometimes she goes out for hours. It's completely unpredictable."

I noticed that Sybil had changed to blues and greens. I suppose she was the kind of woman who looked good in almost anything, but in this gardener's opinion she should have stuck with red.

"And just what do you mean by that?" Tragg was saying to Pierre.

"Exactly what I said," answered the suave Tumblar.

"Have you all just come from a party?" asked Sybil.

"Why do you ask that?" asked Jonathan.

"Because you're in tuxedoes, and Beth there is in a formal gown."

"Life," said Pierre, "is a party. We'd be glad to issue you an invitation."

"No, really," said Sybil.

"We always dress this way when we go out in the evenings," said Joel. "We're the Knights Tumblar. It's our way, you see."

"Well I don't see," said Tragg.

"I'll admit it's a concept that some minds find hard to grasp," said Pierre, "but—"

"Anyway," said Edward, who was still standing before us on the porch, "we just came by so I could drop off these books I borrowed last week from Father's study. I've been meaning to return them, and I hope they weren't missed."

"Ah," I said, taking them one at a time. "*The Incorruptibles* by Joan Carroll Cruz, DuBlanc's *Martyrs of the Catholic Faith,* and one worn volume from one of Father's encyclopedias. You have been busy."

His errand performed, Edward bowed slightly and retreated down the stairs. He paused, then said, "We're having a little get-together at Arthur's tomorrow night. Kahlúa Hummingbird will be there—you remember Pierre's editor at the *L. A. Artsy.* Dinner, drinks, conversation, that sort of thing. We hope Beth will have a few lucid moments."

"We'll try to make it," said Father, "but with all that's going on I can't make any promises."

"Dinner at eight," said Edward, "and who knows after that?"

He turned and joined his friends at the car just as Sybil and Tragg passed him on their way toward us.

"Curious fellows," said Sybil, smiling. "Sergeant Wickes mentioned them a few times. Some sort of Catholic men's club?"

"Something like that," said Father, motioning her inside.

"You've got some weird friends," mumbled Tragg as he sauntered through the doorway.

I watched Arthur's station wagon pull away from the curb before I closed and locked the door. Then I hobbled my way down the hall and turned into Father's study.

Sybil had unknowingly taken my favorite chair, and Tragg its twin. So, having set the books Edward had returned on the edge of Father's desk, I propped myself against the bookcase with my right elbow hooked on the "To be forewarned" shelf, just in front of a volume of misleading drivel entitled *Is Feeneyism Catholic?* by François Laisney. I felt disenfranchised.

"Yes," Father was saying, "Mr. Slater's altar stone is still here in my desk drawer. No, I don't need to open the drawer to make sure because I just removed my pipe from that very drawer a few minutes before your arrival."

"You understand," said Sybil, "that since Mr. Slater is still unconscious—"

"We have no way of verifying your statement that he gave you that stone," said Tragg.

"And you have no way of controverting it, either," said Father. "You know, Sybil, I think I liked it better when you were just a name on a memo. You and your partner here keep barging in upon us, here and elsewhere, and plying us with veiled remarks."

"Oh, you think so," said Tragg. "You—"

"I realize," said Father, "you're playing 'good cop, bad cop.' I used to resort to that silliness myself at one time, but enough is enough. We're on the same side. If you want to know something, ask. And when I want to know something in return, just tell me."

"Hold on," said Tragg, leaning forward in his seat, "you're in no position—"

"No," countered Father, "*you're* in no position. You're in no position to treat me like some clueless pedestrian out for a stroll. I was a cop once, and a good one. I know the ropes. Now, I haven't insisted that you address me as 'Father' because I thought it would just cause friction. But you're not close enough to me to call me anything else, so you give it some thought."

Tragg swallowed loudly.

"And another thing," said Father, leveling a finger directly at Tragg. "Don't you make insinuations about my relationship with Willie Kapps. True, I saved him from the gas chamber by proving he was involved in a seance scam. We weren't yet friends at the time. That's the way the facts fell, that's how the case was disposed. Sure, he's not above being grateful to me for saving his hide—though no doubt he would have preferred some other way. But he's paid his debt to society and he's been clean ever since. He may not be your idea of 'Joe Citizen,' but what you don't realize is that, since his release from prison, he's helped me solve several baffling murders. He knows more about the occult than anyone I know, and I know a lot of people with half the alphabet trailing after their names. He may run a bizarre shop—frankly, he's bizarre himself—but he's one of the citizens that you're sworn to protect. He's my friend now, and I give you my word that if you're going to hound him just because you don't understand him, you'll have to go through me. I trust I'm making myself clear."

"Quite," said Sybil, glancing at her partner.

"Lieutenant?" said Father.

Tragg's face, which for a minute there had almost fleshed out, turned into clay again. He smiled, rubbed his chin, and smiled again. "Okay ... *Father*," he said pleasantly. "Whatever you say."

Father sighed long and hard. "All right, so you're here. What is it that you want?"

"We know that you visited Mr. Kapp's store yesterday," said Sybil. "Hours before last night's burglary, I mean. Did he give you any indication that he was in danger?"

"I'm not sure," said Father.

"Meaning?" asked Tragg.

"Meaning I'm not sure," said Father. "When we arrived he was putting a deadbolt on his front door. He seemed agitated. We talked about friendship, trust, and a little about prayer. Then Martin and I left."

"A deadbolt, you say?" said Tragg. "Why would he be putting that on his door?"

"You've seen the neighborhood, Lieutenant. It's not only his place of business, it's his home."

"But he did ask you to come over," said Tragg.

"Yes."

"To talk about friendship, trust, and prayer?"

"Friends don't usually plan their conversations in advance, Lieutenant. Those were some of the topics we covered during the course of the visit."

"And when was the next time you heard from him?" asked Sybil.

"Last night while you were here," said Father. "The call that came in just after Duggo's from the cemetery. Willie wanted me to come over right away."

"I remember you asked the caller if he was in danger," said Sybil.

"And he said he wasn't," said Father. "So I told him I'd get there as soon as I could."

"Why didn't you tell us that he was the caller?" asked Tragg.

"Because you were both acting like a couple of bullies," said Father. "Now, you tell me something. You knew that Martin and I had been to see Mr. Kapps in the afternoon. Were you staking out Willie or tailing us?"

"We can't tell you that," said Sybil.

"I see," said Father, settling back in his chair.

"Back to square one," muttered the gardener, thinking how much nicer it would be to be curled up in a cozy bed with a good murder mystery—or at least sitting in my chair.

"When you returned to his shop last night ... *Father,*" smiled Tragg, "did you notice anything missing? You understand, we can't ask Mr. Kapps because he's still unconscious."

Father said nothing for long moment, perhaps pondering the relative advantages and disadvantages of cooperating with the uncooperative. Finally he said, "When we arrived at the store the door was kicked in and the light was off. I entered in the dark, my primary concern being Willie's safety. Martin here turned on the lights after I had already found Willie behind the counter. No, I didn't notice if anything was missing. There's so much stuff in the place it would be hard to tell."

"And it moves around," I said. Three pairs of eyes turned toward me. "I mean, Willie's always moving stuff around, rearranging his display cases."

"So you didn't notice anything missing?" asked Sybil.

"No," I said.

"Would you tell us if you did?" asked Tragg. Then he smiled his ugliest smile yet. "Or would you defer to *Father* Baptist's judgment as to whether or not you should tell us?"

"That's it," said Father, standing swiftly. "Get out, Lieutenant."

"What?" asked Tragg, his smile slipping clean off his face.

"Out. Now."

"Father," said Sybil, but saw that it was useless. Her partner had crossed one too many lines. "Very well," she said, gathering her purse. "We'll be going."

"Stay or leave as you like, Sybil," said Father, "but your partner goes."

"Okay," said Tragg, "we'll leave for now. But we'll be back."

"Then come with a warrant," said Father, "because I'll not let you into my house again without it."

After seeing our guests out the front door, I returned to the study to further ponder what book I should grab on my way to that cozy bed I mentioned a few paragraphs back. I was trying very hard not to think about that pouch Willie had placed in Father's keeping, what it might contain, or what the police might conclude if they knew about it.

"Father Baptist," I said, having stooped and chosen Erle Stanley Gardner's *The Case of the Caretaker's Cat* from the plethora of choices on the floor.

"Yes, Martin?"

"Did you mean that?"

"Did I mean what?"

"The bit about them not coming back without a warrant."

"Did I sound like I did?"

"Yes."

"Then that is sufficient."

"But did you?"

"Did I what?"

"Did you mean it?"

"About them not coming back?"

"Without a warrant."

"Enjoy your book, Martin."

"Good night, Father."

"Good night, Martin."

Monday, November Thirteenth

**Feast Day of Saint Homobonus,
who achieved sanctity in the secular life
as a husband and merchant, and died during Matins
at the Church of Saint Giles (1197 AD)**

17

"WHAT'S ALL THIS?" ASKED HAVERMEYER.

"Why, it's your breakfast, Monsignor," said Millie sweetly. "You do like omelets, don't you?"

Father Baptist and I looked from our simple bowls of oatmeal to the bulging omelet on our distinguished associate's plate. Actually, it wasn't just a plate. It was a roast-sized platter, one with vein-like grooves and a catch-basin for the juice, the one Millie inherited from her beloved Great-Aunt Carmella, and it was overflowing with potatoes, bell peppers, and grilled onions—none of them leftovers, by all appearances.

"I don't understand," said the monsignor, dizzy from the fumes as well as the turn of events.

"It's a gift," said Millie, returning to her stove to resume her one-woman war against serenity. "Some of the parish ladies donated the ingredients," she called over her shoulder, "from their own gardens, don't you know, in honor of your first Latin Mass."

"But, I could never eat all this—"

"Shhhhh," shushed the gardener. "Don't spoil the moment. What Millie cooks, men eat. Every bite."

"I'm not a child," said Havermeyer.

"Indeed not. But you are a priest within the range of Millie's frying pan."

"But I couldn't possibly—"

Suddenly there was silence. A shadow fell across the table. We all looked up.

"Something wrong?" demanded Millie, hands on hips.

"No," said the gardener, hefting a gob of gooey oatmeal on his quivering spoon.

"Not a thing," said Father, doing likewise.

"It's just that—" started Havermeyer, eyes darting between his plate and her eyes.

"Just what?" said Millie, biceps bulging.

"—I'm overwhelmed," said Havermeyer meekly.

She smiled an ominous grin, then shot back to her stove. There was a pan on the back burner that she apparently hadn't terrorized with a spatula yet.

"Feeney," whispered Havermeyer, "help me."

"Not on your life," I said around a mouthful of oatmeal.

"I'll burst."

"We all have our Crosses to bear."

"By the way," said Father, "I notice that Joel hasn't been dining with us since Saturday morning. What's going on with him?"

"Obviously," said Millie, "he's helping his friends take care of Arthur's poor sister."

"Ah," said Father, "of course."

GARDENING TIPS: Joel Maruppa, the youngest Tumblar, lived in a spare room up-
stairs. He had fled the archdiocesan
seminary to move in with us. He was
earning his keep by rewiring and remodeling several rooms on the upper floor.
His grandfather, Josef, was helping him.
The old man vacillated between our rectory and the Maruppa family home in Bark-
inbay Beach. Joel and Josef had become

irregular but valued members of our cozy
parish family.

                                        --M.F.

Just then the phone rang.

"Better get it, Martin," said Father.

"But," I said, eyeing Millie eyeing me.

"It might be Lieutenant Taper," said Father as the phone chimed a second time.

"Okay," I said, reaching for the receiver. "I don't mind a few broken bones."

"We all have our Crosses," said Havermeyer, gathering up his fork.

"Saint Philomena's," I said. "Yes, Lieutenant. He's right here."

"Larry," said Father, accepting the phone across the table, "I thought it might be you. What have you got?"

Millie rattled a few pots to express her disapproval as Father listened, slowly rolling a wad of oatmeal around his mouth.

"Okay," he said at last, gulping audibly. "That should prove to be enlightening. Martin and I will be over as soon as we finish breakfast."

He handed me the receiver and I tossed it into its cradle.

"What," I said, scooping up another spoonful of sludge, "is going to enlighten us this morning?"

"Apparently," said Father, "all the security guard's radio communications at the cemetery are recorded on tape. I guess Roberto and Duggo weren't aware of that or they'd surely have said something. Roy Malloy, one of the guards they filled in for the other night, just brought the tape to Larry's office."

"So the murder was recorded on that tape," I said.

"So it would seem. Well, are you finished, Martin?"

"Yup," I said, shoveling the last load into my mouth.

"What about me?" asked Havermeyer desperately, a mere twentieth of his repast consumed.

"Take your time," I said, grabbing my cane and struggling to my feet. "Don't drink any coffee—it'll only make what's already in your stomach swell—and take long, deep breaths between swallows."

"Welcome to the club," said Father, patting the monsignor on the shoulder. "Where you sit, I once sat."

"And nearly exploded," I added as we headed for the door.

18

"WAIT A MINUTE," CRACKLED THE VOICE of Roger Galloway from the cassette recorder on Lieutenant Taper's desk. *"Something flashed in my beam. I'm going in there to look around."*

Father and I drew close. Taper leaned back in his squeaky chair. Sergeant Wickes was standing by the window, his hands shoved into his hip pockets.

"Come again?" barked Duggo's voice. *"What did you say?"*

"Something ... shiny," whispered Galloway.

There was a rumbling sound, as if something was rubbing against the mouthpiece of the walkie-talkie. Galloway's next words were muffled, coming out something like, *"Aura-or"* or *"Ra-ra-ror."*

"I did not catch that," said Duggo. *"Roger? What is happening?"*

"Hang on," said Galloway.

Then, after a couple more seconds of rubbing and bumping, there was a soft thump followed by a rolling sound and then another thump.

"Damn!" cursed Galloway, clear as a bell. *"I'll get it."* This was followed by some more rubbing sounds, a little grunt, another grunt, *"Almost got it ..."* There was a moment's silence, then what could have been a gasp or a sigh that seemed to turn into a low groan—almost but not quite *"Ohhh."* This moan or whatever was cut off by a sudden hollow thud, followed a second later by a resounding *CLUNK!* that was loud enough to distort the speaker. There was a half-second of rubbing cloth and the settling of stone, and then silence—or rather, tape hiss.

"*Roger?*" said Duggo. "*Roger? Are you okay? Look: hold on. Roberto, he is coming! Roger? Roger—?*"

Taper reached over and shut off the machine.

Father leaned back in his chair, forehead furrowed in thought.

"It corroborates Duggo's story," said the gardener, scratching his chin with the handle of his cane.

"But it doesn't tell us much," said Taper. "Jack?"

"I don't know," said Father. "Do you have photographs of the body as it was discovered?"

"Right here," said Taper, opening a folder and handing Father several glossies across the clutter of his desk.

I shifted closer to get a better look. Yes, it's what I had seen in the alcove two nights before, only that had been dark and indistinct, and this was up close and ugly.

"That's his walkie-talkie clutched in his left hand, which is at his side," said Father. "Notice his right arm is extended toward the empty crypt. The flashlight is against the base of the wall, a good six inches or so from his right hand."

"It probably slipped from his fingers when he fell to the floor," said Wickes.

"Perhaps," said Father. "What's this next to the flashlight? Tiny glass fragments? Was the lens of the flashlight shattered?"

"No," said Wickes. "That's intact. We collected the fragments. They pieced them together in the lab. Don't yet know what they came from. At first we thought it was an optical lens, like maybe from someone's glasses, but it's perfectly round and flat like a poker chip."

"Hmm," hmmed Father.

"Something caught his attention in the alcove," said Taper. "Something that glistened in the dark. And when he went in to investigate, the murderer came up from behind and clubbed him."

"With the marble slab?" asked Father.

"Well, obviously," said Taper, pointing to the top photograph. "It's still there leaning against his head."

"Larry," said Father, "I trained you better than that. That marble stone is two foot square and an inch thick. It's pretty darned heavy. The murderer would have to hold it up with both hands."

"Sure," said Wickes, "like this." He took a stance something like Charlton Heston gripping the Tablets of the Law in *The Ten Commandments.* "Then he just brought it down—so."

"But," said Father, "Galloway's injury was on the back, not the top, of his head."

"So maybe," said Wickes, "the murderer gripped it in front of him and sort of lunged forward, clobbering Galloway from behind."

"But if the murderer did that," said Father, "the slab would be right in front of his face. He'd be lunging blindly."

"Maybe he was startled," said Wickes. "In a panic, people do strange things. Heck, maybe he swung it sideways like a baseball bat."

"I doubt that," said Father. "But even so, having hit Galloway with the slab, considering its weight, wouldn't the murderer have simply dropped it where he stood, or set it aside? Why, after the guard collapsed on the floor, did the murderer then take the stone slab and lay it down in such a way that it was found resting against the dead man's head?"

"I see your point," said Lieutenant Taper.

"I don't," said Wickes.

"Was there a blood stain on the marble slab?" asked Father.

"Yes," said Taper.

"Just one?"

"Uh, yes."

"No other marks of contact—hair, skin, blood—on any other part of the stone?"

"No, just the one bloody stain," said Taper, "round, about three inches in diameter."

"No smudges or smears?"

"Nope."

"And that stain was right where the slab made contact with Galloway's head in death?" asked Father.

"Yes."

Father straightened. "So you think the murder whacked Galloway on the head, which of course left a bloody mark on the stone. Then, when the body had fallen to the floor, he went to the trouble of positioning the stone in such a way that the same bloody mark would be found pressed against the gash on the back of the guard's head? This was done in utter darkness, and again I emphasize that Galloway's injury was on the back, not the top, of his skull."

"That does sound improbable," admitted Taper.

"But what else could have happened?" said Wickes.

"I don't know," said Father. "The last sound on that tape before Duggo sent Roberto to assist is the loud thump when Galloway was struck. I heard no movements after that, did you? No grunting as the murderer set down the stone and positioned it against Galloway's head. If your reconstruction is accurate, we should hear sounds to that effect."

"I repeat," said Wickes, "what else could have happened?"

"What did the Medical Examiner say about the injury?" asked Father. "Was Galloway's skull fractured? Surely if someone walloped him with that slab it could have caved-in his skull."

"He didn't say at the crime scene," said Taper. "Those guys never commit to anything anymore until after the autopsy."

"And when is that scheduled?" asked Father.

"This morning," said Wickes. "'Round eleven. But of course Galloway's skull had to be fractured. That stone, as you pointed out, weighed a ton."

Father smiled. "Well, not a ton perhaps, but ..." Something caught his attention in one of the photographs. "What's this?" he asked, pointing to something resting in the small of Galloway's back, partially hidden by a tuck in the man's shirt.

"Another odd thing," said Taper. "That's a gold ring."

"A ring?" said Father.

"Yeah," said Wickes. "Just a simple gold ring. Probably a man's. No jewels or identifying marks."

"Martin," said Father, turning to me. "Didn't Pierre leave a ring in the crypt?"

"Yes," I said. "When Roberto finished cementing the slab to the wall that morning Pierre left his ring on the top edge. Since the cardinal hadn't seen fit to arrange a plaque for Saint Valeria's new crypt, Pierre put his ring there as a marker so they could find it again."

"Not a very reliable marker," said Wickes. "Anyone who visited the mausoleum could have seen it and taken it."

"But I'll wager a dinner at Darby's that no one did," said Father. "You contact Pierre Bontemps at the offices of the *L. A. Artsy*, and I'll bet he'll identify this as his ring."

"So how did it end up on the back of the corpse?" asked Taper.

"I'm quite sure," said Father, "that Pierre doesn't know the answer to that question."

"I'll wager another dinner on that one," said the gardener. "Not only is Pierre's character above question—and you should know that, Lieutenant, you, too, Sergeant—but he and the Tumblars were in the process of taking Arthur's sister, Beth, home from the airport at the time. Father, you'll remember they dropped by the rectory Saturday night while we were having dinner."

I turned to Lieutenant Taper. "Her name is Beth, and she has narcolepsy—bad."

"Narcolepsy?" asked Wickes.

"It's a sleeping disorder," I explained. "She falls asleep any old time and often, and that's how she was—asleep—in the back seat of Arthur's station wagon."

"Yes," said Taper. "I saw her with the Tumblars yesterday morning at Mass. She was asleep the whole time. So you say that Arthur and the boys brought her by the rectory Saturday evening?"

"She was asleep in the back seat," I said.

"So Arthur woke her up so you could meet her?" asked Taper.

"No," I said. "I guess with severe narcolepsy all you can do is let them sleep. We just saw her in the back seat, out cold. Millie and Monsignor Havermeyer were with us. They can tell you."

"Then what?" asked Taper.

I shrugged. "The Tumblars drove off and we all went back into the rectory. Shortly afterwards Father Baptist, Monsignor Havermeyer, and I retired to the study while Millie finished destroying the dishes. That's when Sybil Wexler and Tragg Holcomb barged in, and Duggo phoned a few minutes later. Galloway was murdered during that phone call."

"How much time elapsed, would you say," asked Taper, "between the Tumblars' departure and Duggo's phone call?"

"Not more than twenty minutes," I said.

"More like fifteen," said Father.

"And there's no way Pierre could have gotten from the rectory to New Golgotha in that amount of time," I said. "It takes at least a half hour in good traffic. Saturday evening downtown, it would take a lot longer."

Taper and Wickes looked satisfied. I felt pretty proud of myself for putting all that together in my head without assistance. But suddenly I became aware that Father Baptist was shaking his head.

"Martin," he said at last. "That's all fine except for one thing."

"What's that?" I asked.

"Pierre wasn't with the Tumblars when they came by the rectory."

"What's that?" asked Wickes. "What did you say?"

"Not that it means anything," said Father, "but Martin is mistaken about that. When we went out to the car to meet Arthur's sister, Joel and Jonathan were leaning against the car. Edward was fiddling with the luggage rack on the roof—Beth's wheelchair had slipped or something. But Pierre wasn't with them."

"You're sure," said Taper.

"Very," said Father, glancing down at the photographs of the dead security guard, still in his hand.

"What do you have to say about that, Martin?" asked Taper.

Let me tell you, this ol' gardener's brain was going through a meat grinder, trying to remember if Pierre had been in the back seat of the station wagon with Beth. Pierre was so much a part of what made the Tumblars the Tumblars, it was hard to imagine them without him. Still, the more I thought about it, the more I realized Father was right.

"I guess Pierre wasn't with them," I said at last.

"Don't look so worried, Martin," said Father. "You know as well as I that Pierre didn't kill Galloway. He was off doing something else—procuring a case of champagne for the evening or something."

"Mr. Bontemps works at the *L. A. Artsy*," said Taper. Uh-oh. *Mister* Bontemps. The lieutenant was turning official with respect to Pierre. Not a good sign. "What about the other Tumblars?"

"Pierre could give you all that," said Father. "Phone numbers and all. Call the *Artsy*. Now, before Martin and I head for the hospital to see Archibald Roring, would you mind playing that tape for me one more time? I'd like to get the sequence of sounds fixed in my mind."

"Sure, Jack," said Taper, punching some buttons on the cassette machine. "No problem."

Play the tape? I gawked silently. What about Pierre? What about—?

"Wait a minute," crackled Roger Galloway's voice presently. *"Something flashed in my beam. I'm going in there to look around ..."*

The tape rolled on, Galloway died once again, but this gardener wasn't listening.

19

"I TELL YOU I DON'T REMEMBER," said Archibald Roring, rolling his head from side to side in his hospital bed.

"You don't remember being found by the police at the cemetery that night?" asked Father.

"Well, yes."

"And you told them you were hiding?"

"Um, yes. I remember that."

"And what were you hiding from?"

Roring's mouth started to form a word, but then collapsed.

"You won't tell me?" asked Father.

"You wouldn't believe me."

Father straightened and looked at me with those unnerving eyes that seemed to whisper, penetrating yet patiently, "Considering all that I do believe, Martin, does this confused fellow really think he could come up with something that is beyond me?" I'd seen that look before and knew it well. But all he finally said was, "Well, I guess that's it for now."

We were almost out the door when Roring called out, "Father Baptist. You said something when you came to see me in my office, something about you only saying the Latin Mass at your parish."

Father stopped and turned. "That's right."

"How do you get away with it? I mean, Cardinal Fulbright can't stand anything that even hints at Tradition."

"That's a long story," said Father.

> GARDENING TIPS: Indeed it is ... a very
> long story. So long, I wrote a book
> about it--but that, too, is a long story.
> Publishers, how we wuvs them!
>   I will tell you this: Father Baptist
> "gets away with it" because he has some-
> thing on Cardinal Fulbright, and the
> something he has is in his gardener's
> safe deposit box. When in Rome, and all
> that. As Perry Mason once said in The
> Case of the Golddigger's Purse, "There's
> a lot of blackmail in the world."
>   It works, you see. That's its charm.
>   --M.F.

"I'd like to hear it," said Roring.

"And I'd like to hear what you saw in the cemetery last night," said Father.

"I was drunk."

"*In vino veritas,*" said Father. "In wine there is truth."

"I was drinking martinis."

"All the better," said the gardener. "In gin and vermouth there is honesty."

"You left Darby's between seven and seven-thirty," said Father. "You drove to the cemetery. Your car was found parked on the street just outside the gate. When Martin and I came to your office around five o'clock Saturday afternoon, there was a newspaper on your desk. You had circled an article about the transfer of Saint Valeria's relics to the mausoleum. Why did you go there?"

"I was angry," admitted Roring. "My father had a great devotion to Saint Valeria. On the heels of Father Upshaw selling Dad's monstrance to that pawnbroker, it was just too much."

"I repeat," said Father. "Why did you go there?"

"To pray," said Roring. Then he gulped audibly. "Maybe ... to apologize."

"Well said. So you climbed the gate and headed for the mausoleum."

"The gate wasn't locked," said Roring. "It was closed, and the chain was wrapped around the poles, but the lock was hanging open."

"Indeed," said Father. "That's very interesting. So you let yourself in through the gate, set the chain back in place, and—I repeat—you went to the mausoleum."

"Y-y-yes," stammered Roring.

"You went inside?"

"I was going to."

"What stopped you?"

"As I was approaching the entrance I saw something—some *things*—coming out."

"What things?"

"You wouldn't believe me."

Father sighed. "Okay, you saw some *things* that you assume I'll refuse to accept. Then what did you do?"

"I dove for the cover of the grave markers. The mausoleum is situated in the older part of the cemetery where they still have those big stone monuments."

"And then what happened?"

"I must have hit my head, or just passed out. The next thing I knew, there was this cop standing over me."

"You're aware that a guard was killed in the mausoleum last night?"

"The police told me."

"And that's all you have to say?"

"That's all I *can* say ... um ... unless you're willing to hear my confession."

"No," said Father. "As far as I can tell, you're not in immediate danger of death. I'm investigating a crime, and I can't put myself in the position of getting information that way because I'd be unable to act upon it. You can summon the hospital chaplain, or I can send over my associate, Monsignor Havermeyer, if you'd prefer. But if you won't tell me what you saw at the mausoleum that night, I'll have to find out some other way."

"I'll think about it," said Roring, sinking against his pillow.

"You do that," said Father. "Martin, we've got a busy day ahead of us."

"Coming," I said, nodding to Archibald Roring. "We're in the phone book, you know. Saint Philomena's. Feel free to call the rectory any time."

But Archibald Roring was slowly shaking his head no.

Father took ten seconds to look in on Willie "Skull" Kapps in his room up on the third floor, but the man who had placed his trust in Father Baptist was still unconscious. Mr. Slater, across the hall, was in the same shape.

"Where to now?" I asked as we stepped into the elevator.

"Saint Barbara's Chapel."

"Why there?"

"That was the residence of the late Bishop Jeremiah Ravenshorst. I want to look at his files if they haven't been placed in storage. The information on those cards from Cardinal Fulbright's trophy case was pretty sparse. I want to see if Jerry knew more than he let on when he typed them."

"Or than the cardinal was willing to let on."

"You get the idea," said Father.

"Sure," I said, not at all sure that I did.

20

SAINT BARBARA'S CHAPEL AROUSED MEMORIES of saner times, at least when viewed from the outside. It was built when churches were still constructed of brick and mortar instead of girders and pipes, and the stained-glass windows depicted Saints performing heroic deeds rather than deranged artisans suffering from acid indigestion. Inside, however, the fruits of post-conciliar renewal came to the fore. The arched ceilings had been sealed off with suspended acoustic panels and the masonry overlaid with flat gray paint. Statues of Saints had been replaced with unrecognizable geometric sculptures, and something resembling a giant tic-tac-toe grid had been substituted for Christ on the Cross. Like so many Catholic Churches in Los Angeles, all trace of traditional form and practice had been removed to accommodate the New Liturgy. On this sad description I shall not tarry.

Besides, during the catastrophe the previous June, the inside had been damaged considerably—the word "gutted" would apply—by an electrical event in which several people lost their lives. Monsignor Havermeyer had escaped with permanent disfigurement. The church building was still closed to the public, the funds for remodeling not yet accumulated. A sign by the door suggested that the parishioners seek religious resolve at one of several listed churches. I noticed that they weren't all Catholic.

The woman who answered the rectory doorbell was not delighted by our intrusion.

"You'll have to get the cardinal's permission," she said curtly, "to go through Jerry's files."

"I have it," said Father. "You can call the Chancery for verification, if you like. I take it that the files are still in his library?"

"Yes, but I don't think he'd appreciate you messing them up."

"Who?"

"'Scuse me?"

"You don't think who would appreciate me going through the files?"

"Why ... Jerry."

"Bishop Jeremiah, may he rest in peace, is in no position to object," said Father. "And as I said, I'm working for Cardinal Fulbright."

She shrugged irritably and stepped aside.

"Thank-you," said Father. "We know our way."

Bishop Ravenshorst's library hadn't changed since the last time we had been there the previous June. Twenty of Father Baptist's studies could have been packed inside with room to spare. The walls were lined with shelves, and the shelves were brimming with leather-bound books. Prominent in the room was a huge table over thirty feet in length, still piled with manuscripts, folders, scrolls, legal tablets, and scattered writing utensils. Draped over all this was a layer of dust. No one, it seemed, had taken an interest in Bishop Ravenshorst's research since his demise.

"So how do you expect to find anything in all of this?" I asked, leaning against the edge of the table.

"Simple," said Father, strolling purposefully over to a set of filing cabinets. He located a certain drawer and pulled it open. "I'm going to look under 'R' for 'Relics.'"

"Sure," I said. "Sure."

"Here we are," he said almost immediately, pulling a bulging folder out by the roots.

"You're kidding."

"Have it your way," he said, walking over to the table. With a backhanded sweep he cleared some space, set the file down, and let it spill open. With deft fingers he began riffling through the layers of mismatched papers and certificates.

Within minutes he had found what he was looking for.

"You don't happen to see a photocopier around here, do you?" he asked. "That woman would never let us take these with us, not without raising a ruckus."

"You are acting under the cardinal's authority," said I. "That can be confirmed with a phone call."

"A call that would draw attention to our activities. I'd rather avoid that."

"Gotcha. Uh, that's a 'no' on the photocopier."

"Well, I'll just have to take notes for the nonce."

He found a slab of foolscap, a ballpoint that still wrote, and seated himself like a gourmet at a seven-course banquet. Figuring he'd be a while, I grunted my way into a high-backed wooden chair and rested my hands on the handle of my cane.

"Here's a report on Cardinal Fulbright's precious chalice," said Father after a while, "the one given to him by Professor Murkenstein. As I thought, it has no history other than its commission and manufacture in Pittsburgh."

"Does it say anything," I asked, "about it purposely being made ugly?"

"No, but according to this note clipped to this report—I think it's in Bishop Ravenshorst's handwriting—the cardinal consigned it almost immediately to his trophy case."

"He never said Mass with it?"

"Apparently not."

"Odd."

"Not for Morley Fulbright."

"So what does that tell you?"

"Nothing I hadn't already surmised." He shifted his attention to several brittle onionskin sheets, old carbons apparently, that were stapled at the upper left corner. "Now here we have something interesting ... most interesting."

"Do tell."

"*Le San Pres'que Grall,*" said Father, snatching up a pen and jotting notes. "The other chalice that was stolen, the one Cardinal Fulbright dismissed as inconsequential due to its questionable authenticity. The card Bishop Ravenshorst typed for the cardinal's trophy case simply said, 'An ancient cup which may trace its origin to 1st century Palestine. Presented by the Carmelite Nuns of Port Tobacco, Maryland, to Francis McInery in 1940 upon his appointment as Archbishop of Los Angeles.'"

"I assume you've found something more."

"A lot more. Apparently the chalice has quite a history. Several medieval scholars placed it at the Last Supper. Their argument—I must look up these sources at the library—wasn't over its authenticity, but rather whether it was used by Saint John or Saint Peter the night before Christ's Crucifixion."

I felt that peculiar prickle of hairs rising to attention in various regions of my scalp. "Do you mean ... are you telling me ... that it once held ...?"

"No, there was never any claim that it held the Precious Blood, but it was believed to be part of the tableware used at the Last Supper. The followers of Jesus took pains to preserve many articles from the events surrounding Christ's Passion and Death."

"Hmm," I hmmed. "You mean like the Holy Grail."

"The Holy Grail was taken to England by Joseph of Aramathea, and eventually found its way to Valencia where it still resides."

"Not according to all the Holy Grail movies."

"Hollywood never has been keen on history, Martin. But that's another story. We're concerned with *Le San Pres'que Grall*. My French isn't so bad after all: 'The Holy next to the Grail.' It no doubt stood just inches away from the Holy Grail on the table in the Cenacle when Christ said the First Mass."

"So did the 'next to' accompany the 'actual' to England?"

"No." He flipped to the next page. "According to this, it remained in Palestine until Saint Helena, Constantine's mother, brought it to Constantinople along with other relics of the Passion. It was stored at Santa Sophia until 1203 when the Crusaders took it. The next entry is a reference to its sale in 1230 by Emperor Baldwin—you'll recall he was Emperor of Constantinople during the eighty years that the Latins controlled the region before the Byzantines took the city back."

"Of course," I said, recalling no such thing; but I didn't want to interrupt the flow with my lack of knowledge.

"Emperor Baldwin sold it to the King of France along with the Crown of Thorns."

"Excuse me, Father, you say that the Emperor *sold* it to the King of France?"

"Well," said Father, turning another page, "let's just say he gave it as collateral for a loan he didn't expect to repay. King Louis—*Saint* Louis IX—understood the arrangement. We know that he built Sainte Chapelle specifically to house the Crown of Thorns."

"Okay," I said, more hairs rising to attention. "What next?"

"The 'next to,' as you called it, remained in Sainte Chapelle until the French Revolution, when the zealots desecrated the churches. They had a particular passion for destroying relics. Many were secreted by the faithful in Notre Dame Cathedral. This cup—'the least sacred of all'—disappeared about that time. One chronicler reported a rumor that it was stolen during one of the revolutionary raids, but that's just speculation."

"We're still a long way from Cardinal Fulbright's private chapel."

"We're getting there, Martin, we're getting there. The 'next to' showed up in an auction house in London in 1830—not even a hint as to how it made its way across the Channel. In any case, it was purchased by one Kenelin Digby, a Catholic layman whose shipping business took him back and forth across the Atlantic. It was he who gave it to the Carmelite Convent in Port Tobacco, Maryland, where—get this—it was used at Mass in their chapel."

"In that sense," said the gardener, "you could say it eventually did hold the Precious Blood."

"Well put," smiled Father. "The nuns in turn gave it to Francis McInery when he was appointed Archbishop of Los Angeles in 1940. McInery was a great collector of relics."

"Ah," I said. "So now we've finally arrived at Cardinal Fulbright's trophy case. He inherited the 'next to' from his predecessor."

"Yes," said Father, snatching up another loose sheet. "And here's something intriguing. Those four reliquaries that were also stolen from the cardinal's dwindling collection—I say 'dwindling' because he himself admitted to selling off sacred vessels—those reliquaries containing Saints Athanasius, John Chrysostom, Augustine, and Pope Gregory the Great. Those reliquaries were given to Archbishop Francis McInery in 1953 by none other than ..."

"Does this pause deserve a drum roll?"

"You tell me. Those reliquaries were donated by Themolina Hubbard, heiress to the Roundhead Manhole Cover fortune."

I resisted the impulse to perform a four-stroke ruff and a flam with my tongue.

"And here's something else," said Father. "The vessels which Cardinal Fulbright recently sold—remember that empty shelf in his trophy case—were purchased by one Roderick Roundhead, Themolina's great nephew."

"That would also make him Elza's great nephew," observed the gardener.

> GARDENING TIPS: Ah, the things my reader would already know if my books were in print!
>
> Themolina Hubbard donated the Cordova Homestead Estate on Chapel Hill to the archdiocese when she suffered and sur- vived a heart attack. The ruins of the Del Agua Mission were later discovered on that estate--ruins which figured promi- nently in my book, The Endless Knot. It was during a dedication ceremony at those ruins that Cardinal Fulbright received the bump on his forehead that he so likes to rub.
>
> Themolina's sister, Elza Maplewood Roundhead, played a significant and syn- opsis-resistant role in the sequel, The Darkness Did Not. She was a stand-in pi- anist of sorts at a magic club called "House of Illusions" when the regular guy, Buzz Sawr, was downing some illu- sions of his own at the bar. But that, like so much else, is another story.
>
> --M.F.

"Martin, go over to the window and tell me what you see."

"Come again?"

"Turn away," said Father.

"What?"

Father exhaled in exasperation. "I don't want you to see what I'm going to do with this receipt."

"Oh, sure." With great strain and pain, I got up and lumbered over to the window, oblivious to the sound of old, dry paper be- ing creased, folded, and slipped inside the mysterious folds of

Father's cassock. "Hm," I mused half aloud, "those Roundheads sure do keep popping up in archdiocesan affairs." Then I thought of Elza Maplewood Roundhead. "And sometimes, not so circuitously, in mine."

> GARDENING TIPS: To be fair, my reader will not suffer in the least from not having read those other books of mine. But this new bit of information sure made the present story all the more intriguing from my point of view.
>
> --M.F.

"All clear?"

"Yes, Martin."

"Does that conclude our business here?"

"I think so ... Oh, wait a minute." He took up an old, battered sheet of typing paper. It had been punctured through all over by one of those old typewriters with sharp hammers. "This looks like a rough draft of some copy for a brochure or something. A little background on Saint Valeria's relics."

"Do tell," I said, lurching back to the table.

"Back in 1874 a cathedral was under construction here in Los Angeles. The proposed name was 'Our Lady of the Angels.' But, out of the blue, Pope Pius IX decided that the City of Angels needed a Patron Saint worthy of an expanding metropolis in this swiftly growing country. So the pope arranged for the transfer of the holy relics of Saint Valeria from her resting place in the cathedral named after her in Rome to the new cathedral here. The name of our cathedral was changed appropriately."

"I wonder how the people of Rome felt about that."

"Not very agreeable, according to this. She had been venerated there for many centuries. There was considerable public outcry at the pope's announcement, even some rioting. Still, the pope had the authority, and exercise it he did. Considering the missionary history of California, he felt assured that her relics would be well cared for by the Angelenos."

"Well, the joke was on him, wasn't it?"

"In fact," said Father, glancing again at the page, "such was the wording of his order, that Saint Valeria would, quote, 'be properly protected and adored by the pious people of the City of Angels,' unquote. The pope's very words."

He punctuated the last three words by tapping the battered page with his finger.

"I think," he said, "I'm going to suggest to the Tumblars that they begin a novena to Saint Valeria at once. We'll be seeing them this evening, don't forget."

"No, I haven't forgotten. But something tells me the evening is a long way off."

"You're so right, Martin," said Father, rising. "I couldn't have said it better myself."

21

"SPEAKING OF RELIQUARIES," I said as I parked the Jeep behind the black-and-white unit in front of Willie's shop, "I forgot to mention something I noticed when we were here Saturday afternoon."

"What was that?" said Father, pausing with his hand on the door handle. It rattled loosely beneath the damaged deadbolt as he turned it.

"I noticed four reliquaries in one of Willie's display cases."

"Uh-oh. Did you see which Saints they contained, if any?"

"No, I didn't."

"Well, the police are here now. I'll keep them occupied. Be inconspicuous—"

"Me?"

"—but try to get a close look."

"I'll do my best."

"And don't say anything in their presence."

"Gotcha."

Police tape, which had been temporarily detached to allow the investigators entry, fluttered in the doorway as we stepped inside Willie's establishment.

"Oh, hello Father," said Sybil, looking up from an assortment of withered things spread out on a counter top. Today she was wearing browns and blacks. Nope, red was still her color. "What brings you here?"

"Not that you're welcome," said Tragg, emerging through the doorway connecting the store with Willie's living quarters. The opening was curtained with strings of multicolored beads that waved and rattled as the Lieutenant came toward us.

"We were just passing by," said Father, "and I wanted to make sure that Willie's store was all right."

"Not to worry," said Tragg. "No one's going to rob the place while we're here."

"I can't ask for more than that," said Father. "May I inquire as to what you're doing?"

"We're just taking an inventory—" said Sybil.

"None of your damn business—" said Tragg at the same time.

"An inventory?" said Father. "Why, that's absurd."

"How so?" snapped Tragg, no attempt at his usual smiling exercises. "We've got a warrant."

"To get that you needed a suspicion," said Father. "Of what are you suspicious?"

"It's just routine, Father—" said Sybil.

"Of your so-called friend," said Tragg simultaneously. "I wouldn't be surprised if we found all kinds of illegal substances and stolen merchandise here."

"I see," said Father, glancing at me, then going over to the counter where Sybil was sorting unfamiliar thingamajiggers, "and has your search proved fruitful?"

"Not so far—" said Sybil.

"None of your—" said Tragg.

"You call this an inventory?" scoffed Father, picking up the pad of paper on which she had been writing. "'Three dark objects that appear to be withered hands ... five medallions bearing star-shaped mystic symbols ... three daggers of various lengths ...' You'll pardon me for asking, but how can you two conduct an inventory when you don't even know what it is that you're itemizing?"

"I'm doing the best I can—" said Sybil.

"What the Hell do you know about it?" spat Tragg at the same time.

"I'll show you what I know," said Father, pointing. "Those are monkey paws from Tahiti, not hands."

"I didn't say they were human," said Sybil.

"You left the implication dangling," said Father. He started picking up the medallions. "This is a pentagram, this a hexagram, a dodecagram, a Seal of Solomon, and a medal of Our Lady of Guadalupe."

Acting like I was ducking for cover, I cowered near the display case where the ominous reliquaries resided.

"Now for the daggers," Father was raging eloquent. "This is a scrying knife used in divination, this is a skellkurg—"

"A what?"

"See?" said Father, holding up the glistening implement. "Neither side of the blade is sharpened and the point is nubbed. Definitely a skellkurg, probably from Denmark. And this last 'dagger,' as you listed it, is the letter opener I gave Willie for Christmas last year."

"Oh my—" said Sybil.

"If you're so smart," said Tragg, pointing up to something draped on the wall, "what's that?"

"That," said Father, "is known as a 'casting cloth' or 'witch's quilt.' Willie has quite a collection. It was his knowledge of such quilts that helped me break the Cheryl Farnsworth case last June."

"Tragg," said Sybil, "maybe Father has a point—"

"Officer Wexler," countered Tragg, "we have a job to do, and Father Baptist is interfering. He would be well advised to leave the premises before I arrest him for obstruction."

"Suit yourself," said Father. "As I said, I just wanted to make sure that Willie's store is safe. Martin?"

"Here," I said, having by then wandered over to a rack of crystalline luck charms.

"We're leaving," said Father.

"I'm sorry—" said Sybil.

"Good!" barked Tragg.

"Oh," said Father before exiting, "I would advise you to be very careful in the wording of any official report or arrest warrant that you make, if it comes to that. You wouldn't want me to be called on the witness stand to refute your testimony. I'd make you look foolish."

"Oh, we wouldn't—" said Sybil.

"If that's a threat—" huffed Tragg.

"Merely a fact," said Father, stepping through the doorway.

22

"EXCUSE ME, FATHER," I VENTURED as I pulled the Jeep away from the curb and headed down the street.

"Yes, Martin?"

"A skellkurg?"

"Well, I had to think fast."

"But a *skellkurg?*"

"The syllables just seemed to arrange themselves in my head."

"Oh."

"So tell me, Martin."

"Tell you what, Father?"

"Tell me about the reliquaries."

"Oh, those."

"Yes, those."

"Well, as far as I could tell—you know how small the printing is inside those reliquaries—our friend Willie is harboring such wanted criminals as Saint Peter Claver, Saint Martin de Porres, Saint Rose of Lima, and Saint Anthony Mary Claret. All of them are associated with the Caribbean and South America—like Willie, sort of."

"Whew," said Father. "That's one suspicion laid to rest. I missed a hunch there, but I'm glad Willie wasn't receiving stolen merchandise—especially the cardinal's stolen merchandise."

"You provoked Sybil and Tragg," I commented. "You sure you want them as enemies?"

"Me? I'm not afraid of them, and I think Sybil's a good egg who's been yoked with a bad partner. I hope his attitude doesn't rub off on her."

"Yeah," I nodded. "Me, too. And now?"

"Now, my friend," said Father, "we need to stir up the fire."

"Sounds dangerous."

"It might prove to be."

"Okay," I grimaced, "but before I get my fingers burned, please tell me why we're going to do whatever it is we're going to do—just so that when I'm on my knees before the Blessed Mother I'll know exactly what I'm whining about."

"I would be tempted to concentrate on the theft of Saint Valeria," said Father, "except now we know the significance of *Le San Pres'que Grall* which is of considerable historical value as well. I suspect there's a connection."

"And the cardinal's precious Murkenstein mug?"

"That's just it, Martin. Why would the thief—assuming he knew what he was about—why would he take *both* chalices? The 'next to the Grail,' sure; but Cardinal Fulbright's silly cup?"

"Maybe the thief didn't know what he was about."

"But he also took the four reliquaries, vessels in which reside the relics of Saints Athanasius, John Chrysostom, Augustine, and Pope Gregory the Great—four Great Doctors of the Universal Church. Oh, our thief knew exactly what he was about, I assure you."

"Okay, so how do we stir up the fire?"

"First, pull up to the next telephone booth you see. I want to put a call through to Mr. Roderick Roundhead. If Saint Anthony is with us, Themolina's great nephew just might be able to fit us in without an appointment. Then, I need to ask something of you … Wait a minute, Martin. You just passed a phone booth."

"Yeah," I said, "but I could see that the directory was missing."

"Ah, you're growing observant in your middle age. Okay, I'll leave that up to you. As I was about to say, I'm going to ask you to risk something that is very precious to you."

"Such as?"

"Such as the chip from the Crown of Thorns that Bishop Xandaronolopolis gave you."

"Wow." Precious was right. There was nothing among my material possessions that I considered more priceless and personal than the Maronite bishop's parting gift. "What could you possibly want with that?"

"We need a relic—a genuine relic—something with all the proper authentication papers; enough seals and pedigrees to impress a knowledgeable collector."

"Well, it certainly came with all that. But I thought our thief is interested in big, golden vessels. Bishop Xandaronolopolis gave me the chip in just a tiny holder—so small it didn't even set off the metal detectors at the airport, remember? I haven't yet found a fitting reliquary that I can afford."

"I know where we can probably get one for free."

"Where?"

"You'll see."

"Okay, I don't follow you yet, but okay. What then?"

"Then we use your relic as bait."

"Bait? A chip from the actual Crown of Thorns as bait?"

"It's a risk," he said, "and a big one. I want you to think it over carefully before you answer."

"Oh, I'm with you all the way, Father. You know that. I know you wouldn't do something foolish."

"What do you call getting mixed up in Cardinal Fulbright's little mug hunt?"

"Ahem, as I was saying, I know you wouldn't do something terribly foolish."

"I repeat."

"Well, whatever, Father. I'm with you. But are you going to explain exactly what it is that you plan to do with it?"

"I would if I could, Martin. Murder is my field. I'm improvising as I go on this one. Still, I think a burst of brazen action is in order."

"Well, I'm all for brazen action. Speaking of which, we're about a half-mile from Darby's now. How about some lunch?"

"No time for that, but the lounge there has three payphones and a whole stack of directories. Let's stop wasting our energy looking for phone booths in this neighborhood and go there."

"Speaking of telephones," I said as I changed lanes, "I hope you told Millie we wouldn't be back for lunch."

"Heavens no, Martin. She'll be furious. Tell you what: you call her while I phone Mr. Roundhead."

"Why don't you phone Millie and let me call Mr. Round-head?"

"Because I'm the one doing the improvising, and that's how my plan is formulating itself."

"Oh, of course. How silly of me."

23

THE HOLLYWOOD HILLS ARE CLUTTERED with houses crammed like sardines on every available inch of space. You could open your window to smell the flowers only to bump foreheads with your neighbor who's doing the same. I find the area claustrophobic, though others would disagree or they wouldn't live there. When you get up around the Hollywood Reservoir, however, things get more spacious, more expansive, more ostentatious, and certainly more expensive. I was relieved when Father's directions brought us to the "more" neighborhood.

After convincing a gate guard with an obnoxious set of rattling keys that we were on the level—he phoned his employer to be sure—we came upon the home of Mr. Roderick Roundhead. Home—did I say home? Mansion is more like it. The sprawling building looked like what the Beverly Hillbillies used to occupy, only more of it. The doorbell sounded like something that belonged atop a cathedral.

"You are expected," said the butler, a courtly gentleman's gentleman by the name of Morgan. He ushered us through a living room nearly as big as the nave of Saint Philomena's. "Please walk this way."

GARDENING TIPS: I had waited all my life
for a doorman, a maitre d', anyone to seriously utter that famous comic line in
my hearing, and it had to be a man who
walked slowly and deliberately, without
so much as a hint of a limp!

                                        --M.F.

"What does Mr. Roundhead do for a living?" whispered the
gardener as we followed in the wake of the straight-backed,
long-striding Morgan.

"If he's as rich as he seems," mouthed Father, "not much."

"Reverend John Baptist," announced Morgan as he opened a
huge maple door and stood to one side, "and Mr. Martin
Feeney."

"Father Baptist," said a barrel-chested man, rising from an
enormous leather chair as we entered what seemed to be a sitting
room. The room was obviously designed for sitting because it
was populated with over a dozen similar chairs. "I've heard
about you."

"And my associate," said Father after shaking Mr. Roundhead's muscular hand.

"Yes, yes," said Mr. Roundhead. "Martin Feeney. You two
made something of a splash in the papers a few months ago. Do
be seated. Would you care for anything to drink? Bourbon?
Scotch?"

"Scotch on the rocks would be fine," said Father.

"Would Glenfiddich suffice?" asked Morgan.

"Excellent," said Father. "Then make it straight up."

"Very good, Father," said Morgan. "And you, sir?"

"Ginger ale for me," said the gardener. "Saint Thomas, Salis-
bury." I paused for effect. "'Blue label,' if you have it."

"Of course, sir," said Morgan, as if the question was absurd.

"Jack Daniels for me," said Mr. Roundhead.

"Very good, sir."

As Morgan silently withdrew, I took a moment to take in our
host. He was much younger than I'd expected—early to mid-
forties, tops. His suit was impeccably tailored, and his finger-

nails manicured. I counted two rings on each hand, each with a different colored gem in a distinctly masculine setting. The man wasn't what you would call handsome, but he certainly took meticulous care of what he had. He had an air about him of a man who gets things done, and who brooks no bungling from those in his employ. He gazed upon us with piercing green eyes, eyes that took in everything, eyes that commanded not only respect, but one's full attention.

"So what can I do for you, Father?" asked Mr. Roundhead.

"I'm investigating a series of thefts of Catholic religious objects," said Father. He paused, then added, "at the request of Cardinal Fulbright."

A strange, circular look rippled under the surface of Roderick Roundhead's square face. The muscles in his neck tensed, causing his cheeks, which were as clean-shaven as an egg, to contract. The change in his expression was subtle but effective.

"And what," he said evenly, "would that have to do with me?"

"Nothing," said Father. "I'm simply running down a few leads, discarding details that don't fit but which need to be cleared up before I do so."

"I don't follow you."

"A number of precious objects have been stolen from the cardinal's residence," explained Father.

"My word," said Mr. Roundhead. "Right from under the old poof's nose?"

Father smiled. "You might put it that way. I certainly wouldn't."

"Sure you would," said Mr. Roundhead, smiling broadly. "I know about you, Father. Saint Philomena's is famous within the Traditionalist Movement."

"Really," said Father. "I wasn't aware."

"Of course you are. Of course you are. How could you not be? Of all the priests in Los Angeles who have cut the cord, so to speak, you're the pinnacle, the summit, the apex, the apogee—"

"I hope," said Father, "that such mistaken assumptions about me are not widespread. I have cut no cord of which I am aware."

"You mean to tell me that you're not a renegade?—that you haven't gone 'independent'?"

"I remain in good standing with my shepherd," said Father, "at least as far as my faculties are concerned. Of course, Cardinal Fulbright and I have our theological differences."

"But you only say the Tridentine Mass, and you still perform all the Sacraments in Latin."

"Oh," said Father, "then you've visited my little parish?"

Mr. Roundhead caught himself before answering. Just then, Morgan appeared with a silver tray full of drinks. My Saint Thomas came in the kind of tall hi-ball glass that went out with good taste around 1958.

"Will there be anything else?" asked Morgan.

"Not at present," said Mr. Roundhead.

"Very good, sir."

"You were saying?" asked Father.

"No matter, no matter," said Mr. Roundhead. "I'm still in the dark as to why you've come to see me."

"Well," said Father, reaching into his cassock and pulling out a folded piece of paper which of course I didn't know he had or how it got there. "As I said, Cardinal Fulbright has asked me to investigate certain thefts from his premises. In the course of my inquiry, I happened upon this receipt in the files of the late Bishop Ravenshorst. It appears that you purchased a number of objects from the cardinal six month ago—"

"Yes, I did," harrumphed Mr. Roundhead. "And at the price I paid I'll bet it was the only time under Fulbright's reign that there wasn't a deficit."

"You may be right. Do you mind if I ask you why you bought them?"

"My family has been Roman Catholic since so far back, we don't know how far back. And since my great-great-grandparents came to California, we've been staunch supporters and builders of the Church. I'll have you know that my family donated or participated in the donation of half the objects I purchased from Old Morley. You might say that they were on loan, in a sense, and I simply got them back. Left to his own devices, Fulbright would have sold them to some foreign art collector, or some social misfit who happened to win the lottery. He wanted cash—that's all. And cash is one thing I have aplenty."

"Ah," said Father. "Then it was he who approached you?"

Mr. Roundhead repeated that strange look again, complete with ripples that never quite broke the surface. "I'd rather not say," he said at last. "And I'm afraid I still don't see the point of this conversation."

"There probably isn't any," said Father, setting down his drink and rising from his chair. "As I said, I was just following up leads. Perhaps we should go."

"Please, Father," said Mr. Roundhead, a tad unsettled, "I did not mean to offend. I don't understand your arrangement with the cardinal—either how you've kept your faculties or why you end up doing investigative work on his behalf—but I want you to know that I respect you most highly. You've no idea how hard the post-Vatican II changes have been on some of us laymen."

"Oh, but I do," said Father. "I was one of 'you laymen' before I became a priest. By the way, I noticed four reliquaries in the cardinal's trophy case. I understand that they were a gift to the archdiocese from your aunt, Themolina Hubbard."

"That's right."

"Would you like to get those back if the opportunity presented itself?"

"Certainly."

Mr. Roundhead didn't blink or do the subliminal face dance that time. If Father was laying a trap, Roderick wasn't taking the cheese.

After a minute or so of the three of us listening to each other breathe, Mr. Roundhead finally spoke. "Father, you didn't mention what items were stolen from the cardinal's residence."

"No, I didn't. I'm not at liberty."

"I see."

"But I can tell you about another theft that may interest you. It's being kept from the press, you understand, and I expect you to keep the information confidential. It happened Saturday evening."

"Really," said Mr. Roundhead, himself rising from his chair. "What was stolen, and from where?"

"The body of Saint Valeria, from New Golgotha Cemetery."

Now that sent the ol' sub-dermal whirlpools swirling under Mr. Roundhead's cheeks, let me tell you.

"My word," he exclaimed. "I read in the paper that her relics were being transferred to the mausoleum from the cathedral. That was sacrilegious enough—but this! You're serious."

"I am."

"I don't know what to say. I'll have you know that my great uncle Ronald was instrumental in the pope's decision to bring her here over a century ago. I have my contacts within the police department as well as the private sector. Perhaps I can bring pressure—"

"Perhaps you can," said Father. "Perhaps you can."

So much for keeping the information confidential, thought the gardener.

Then, as Father turned to leave, he lifted his right hand in farewell, then said in the same tone of voice one would say, "Nice meeting you," or "'Til next time": *"Le San Pres'que Grall."*

"You, too," said Mr. Roundhead. "I'll have Morgan show you out."

I was tempted to sneeze, "Murkenstein!" but decided not to overplay Father's hand. Sometimes, on rare occasions, I show good sense.

24

"SO?" I ASKED AS WE DROVE past the gate guard, the one with the irritating keys.

"So what, Martin?"

"Was he lying?"

"He certainly was evasive—as was I."

"Have you ever seen him at Saint Philomena's?"

"Why do you ask?"

"Well, he got this strange look when you asked him if he'd ever been there."

"You noticed that."

"Yes, Father, I did. So did he look familiar to you?"

"I thought so, maybe a little bit, but I can't be sure. A man with his money could afford a pretty convincing disguise. Did you notice the second time he got that 'strange look,' as you called it?"

"Sure. When you asked him if Cardinal Fulbright had approached him about buying those sacred objects."

"The problem there," sighed Father, "is that we still don't know if the cardinal asked him or he asked the cardinal."

"How so? Can't you find out?"

"Do you think it would do any good to ask Cardinal Fulbright?"

"I see your point, Father. We're stuck there."

"But only there, Martin. Only there, and not for long."

"Oh goodie. So where to now?"

"Home for a brief stop, then to a pawnshop we both know near 3rd Street and La Brea, and finally to a hotdog stand only I know on Figueroa."

"Is that the lunch we've been postponing?"

"Only by coincidence. 'Ernie's "World Famous" Hotdogs' is where we pour gasoline on the fire."

"Sounds warm and cozy, Father."

"Don't bet on it, Martin."

25

"So?"

"So what, Martin?"

So, having left a questionable impression on Mr. Roderick Roundhead, we drove back to Saint Philomena's only to find a Ford van parked at the curb in front of the rectory. I'd know that van anywhere. The dented front fender, the purple smoke billowing from behind—it had to belong to Edward Strypes Wynd-ham, third-youngest and third-oldest Knight of the Tumblar. Edward was dropping off Joel Maruppa, the youngest Knight. The two of them were standing on the sidewalk next to the van. Edward had left the rattletrap's motor idling. It gurgled and wheezed like an antique wringer washing machine.

"She," I said to Edward as Father and I emerged from the Jeep, "doesn't seem healthy."

Edward and Joel seemed startled or puzzled by my remark. I indicated the smoke belching from the corroded exhaust pipe.

"Oh," said Joel, his face expressing relief. "I thought you were talking about Arthur's sister."

"Needs a tune-up," nodded Edward, kicking the rear tire, "one of these days."

"And how's Beth?" asked Father.

"Asleep," said Edward and Joel together. They looked at each other and smiled uneasily.

"It's weird being around her," admitted Joel.

"Yeah," said Edward. "One second you're talking to her and she's looking you right in the eye, and the next she's in la-la land and you're talking to yourself."

"Then she wakes up a minute later," said Joel, "and she's still back where she left off, and you've got to retrace what you've said to try to get back to where she is in the conversation. It gets old fast."

"I can see why she has a hard time making friends," said Edward. "Poor kid."

"Talking about sleep," said Joel, "I really need some."

"Okay," said Edward. "I'll swing by and pick you up around six. And then it's party-time at Arthur's."

The two young men did a quick but tired cha-cha.

"Later, Joel," said Edward, climbing into his van. "Good-bye Father, Mr. Feeney."

"You are coming to the party, Father?" asked Joel as he and Father and I climbed the front steps after Edward roared off in his van.

"Martin and I are in the middle of a lot of things," said Father, "but I hope we'll be able to at least put in an appearance."

Once inside, Joel waved a sleepy good-bye, then wearily pulled himself arm-over-arm up the stairs to his second-floor room.

"Martin," said Father, "you get your relic, and I'll explain the dinner situation to Millie."

"Good," I said. "It's your turn. I had to explain the lunch situation to her, remember? She was not pleased."

"I'll be brave," smiled Father. "And I think I'll suggest that Monsignor Havermeyer pay a visit to Good Sam. Perhaps he could do Archibald Roring some good."

We went about our separate missions.

"So?" I asked Father.

"So what, Martin?" Father asked me.

So, some twenty minutes later, he and I were parking near the corner of 3rd and La Brea. Dennis Goodman, it turned out, was only too willing to let Father borrow the reliquary which had been left behind when his display window had been pillaged. His mind was on cash, not sacred objects. He must've asked Father three times in the course of the five-minute conversation just when he thought the police would release the envelope containing $20,500 to him.

"I guess that depends," said Father, "provided they catch the culprit, and whether the money is used as State's evidence in a burglary case or a murder trial."

"Murder?"

"In the unlikely event that Norman Slater doesn't make it."

"I hadn't thought of that." Dennis Goodman took a moment to do so. "Poor Norman." Suddenly he clutched his forehead. "It could take months. Maybe years."

"Sorry," said Father. "I wish there was something I could do, but it's out of my hands."

"Then please solve this case as soon as you can," said Goodman. "What am I saying? Of course you will."

"I'll do my best," said Father, shaking his hand in farewell. "Thank-you for the use of this reliquary. You understand that I can't guarantee its safe return."

"You don't have to return it. Consider it yours."

"You are most generous. Oh, and thank-you, too, for the gift of the vestments."

"Norman wasn't supposed to tell you they were from me."

"Well, considering you had called ahead to announce us, who else could it have been?"

"Yeah, I see your point. Use them well, Father, whatever-it-is you do with them."

"You should drop by for Mass and see sometime."

"I might just do that," smiled Goodman, "one of these days."

GARDENING TIPS: "Always put off to tomorrow what you're too lethargic to do today." That's my motto. The bigger the
plan, the more you need to consider it.
Providentially, Father Baptist rarely
lets me live up to this time-honored phi-
losophy.

                                    --M.F.

"So?" I was therefore asking, maybe fifteen minutes after that, which brings us to the heart of this chapter.

"So what, Martin?"

"So, how good are Ernie's 'world famous' hotdogs? This question, you understand, comes from my heart—or rather, from an organ very near it that's panting like a starving mutt."

"I have no idea in what world his cuisine is famous," smiled Father, as I pulled the Jeep into the tiny, angular, lopsided parking lot beside the seediest looking hotdog stand this gardener had ever seen. "But I hope he's our gateway to the underworld—not *the* underworld, let us pray, but perhaps one of the parallel worlds that float just beneath the veneer of this so-called metropolitan community."

I looked at him. "That was a bit on the poetic side."

"I feel like a poet sometimes."

"Oh brother," I said. "I can see the headlines now when Jacco Babs at the *Times* gets wind of this: COP-TURNED-PRIEST-TURNED-COP-TURNED-POET! DON'TCHA KNOW IT? And there'll be a photograph of you standing at the fountain at Griffith Park reading verses to the little people—a photograph that will have been taken by none other than Ziggie Svelte, Jacco's faithful sidekick and winner of this year's 'Strobie' award."

Father paused with his hand on the door handle. "What are you going on about, Martin?"

"Don't mind me. When I get this hungry I get delirious."

"I'm not sure," said Father, indicating the overflowing trash barrels leaning against the side of the crumbling building, "that you want to satiate your hunger here."

Sadly, I watched the flies buzzing merrily around the garbage. "Then what am I to do, Father?"

Father leaned toward me. "Listen, Martin, and listen well: Ernie Corben is one of the most dangerous men I know. I don't believe he's ever committed murder, but he's connected with a lot of people who do. Normally, I would avoid contact with such men, but in my former line of work it was sometimes inevitable."

I looked at him, wondering where this was going.

He looked at me, knowingly. "The fact is—and if you write what I'm about to tell you in one of your novels I'll see to it that Millie feeds you nothing but rat brains for the rest of your life—Ernie's kid sister, a sweet girl named Vicki, was raped by a frightening fellow by the name of Anton Grisler. She notified the police. He was located and brought in. She picked him out of a lineup. Grisler was identified by two impartial witnesses, neighbors who had spotted him stalking her within a block of her home the night of the attack. The judge let him off on a technicality that was so asinine I don't want to repeat it."

"So what happened?" I asked, so hungry I was savoring the thought of braised rat brains smothered in Millie's secret, pungent, rodent purée.

"One evening, a week later, Grisler waited for Vicki in the bushes by her front porch. This time he slashed her with a knife—internally as well as externally. She survived, but it's doubtful she'll ever be able to bear children. Grisler was brought in again, she identified him again, and the judge let him off on another version of the same technicality that got him off the first time."

"Oh, brother."

"It gets better, Martin. At the courthouse steps, Vicki, fearing for her life, begged the nearest policeman to help her. He happened to be a friend of mine on the force, Officer Jesse J. Fontana, who later admitted that when she asked him what was left for her to do, he told her, 'Waste him. We'll look the other way.'"

"Did she?"

"I think so. I suspected as much. Several friends provided her with an alibi, but they were all connected with her unscrupulous brother, Ernie. We did find the gun, but it had been wiped clean. The paraffin test we ran on her was inconclusive. If Ernie had a hand in it, one or more of his pals would have come forward to provide him with an ironclad alibi as well."

"So what did you do?"

"I had to make a judgment call. I decided not to pursue the case. The DA wasn't happy about it, but I told him there was no way we could prove anything beyond a reasonable doubt, not if the jury was apprised of the two previous dismissals and the stalking—and certainly not if Officer Fontana was ever called to the witness stand. No, it was better all around to just drop it. But I did come here and tell Ernie to his face what I believed had transpired, and exactly why I wasn't going to try to build a case against him or his sister."

"And how did he react to that?"

"He simply said, 'Jack, you keep in touch.' I took that to mean—and we're here now because I'm still taking it to mean—that he owed me one."

"A supportable hypothesis," I nodded.

"Well, we're going to find out. I think he'll pay up. He may be a crook, but he's from the old school where a man does what he says he's going to do. Honor among thieves, or whatever. The question is: *can* he help us?"

"Help us to do what?"

"You'll see. You've put the chip from the Crown of Thorns in Mr. Goodman's reliquary? Let me have a look. Good. And you brought the certificate of authenticity? Fine. Well, let's have a talk with Ernie Corben and see where it gets us."

"One last question. If this Ernie is so well-connected, why—?" I completed the sentence by framing the dumpy eatery with my hands.

Father shrugged. "Maybe he just likes to cook."

With that we got out of the car, entered the little joint, and encountered a nasty-looking fellow with an eggplant for a nose and garden snails for eyes.

"Hey, Jack," said the hash slinger, wiping his greasy hands on his slimy apron. "I knew you'd be gettin' in touch someday."

"Ernie," nodded Father, easing himself onto a wobbly stool.

"What's that around your neck?" asked Ernie. "No, don't tell me. I heard you changed professions. You know what? Vicki's never forgotten what you did for her."

"More like what I didn't do."

"Ain't it so? And who's this guy?"

"Martin Feeney, my associate."

I nodded, smiled, and remained standing.

"You want chow?" asked Ernie, indicating his filthy grill.

"Not me," said Father, glancing at me.

"No thanks," I agreed.

"I could use your help," said Father.

"Sure," said Ernie, nodding. "I owe you one, and I pay my debts. Do I have to call you 'Father'?"

"Appropriate, but not vital. We have a religious object here—something very precious to us—that we want to sell."

"Yeah?" said Ernie. "What is it?"

Father motioned, so I produced the reliquary, holding it up for Ernie to see. "It's a relic," I said. "It's a piece of—"

"Real or road kill?" asked Ernie.

"Excuse me?" I asked.

"I went to Cat'lic school when I was a kid—Mamma's idea of a joke. I know what a relic is, or what it's supposed to be. So I'm askin': is it real or rot?"

"Oh, it's real," said Father.

"It's a chip from the Crown of Thorns," I said.

"Go on," said Ernie.

"No, really," I said. "I have the certificate right here—"

"Don't bother," said Ernie. "If it's in Latin, it won't mean nuthin' to me. And even if it's in English, what would I know? Certificates can be counterfeited. Hell, two blocks from here is a guy who could fake anythin'. He can make you a copy of the Declaration of Independence that even the American Historical Society wouldn't question. The Crown of Thorns, eh? I never heard that the thing was still in existence."

"The thing, as you call it," said Father, "resides in Paris at Sainte Chapelle. This chip was a gift from a bishop. I can assure you it's authentic."

"You're serious."

"I am."

"And you wanna sell it?"

"The situation requires it."

"Hmm," said Ernie, scratching his stubble. "Collections must be lean. Okay ... *Father* ... I owe you, so I'll help you. I need to make some calls. I'll phone you when I set somethin' up."

"We're on the move," said Father. "There's no way we can be reached."

"Sure there is," said Ernie, groping down behind the counter. He produced a cell phone. It was grimy. "Keep this with you. I sell 'em on the side, you know. When you hear it beep, press the 'send' button. It'll be me."

"Any idea how long it will take?" asked Father, accepting the crusty implement.

"That I can't tell you, but be ready to roll the minute I call, whenever I call."

"And then?" I asked.

"I'm goin' to put you in touch with whatcha might call a doorman. He's the guy that lets you in. I'll stake my reputation to cover yours, so don't cross me. Once you're with him, you won't need me. Gottit?"

"And what do you want for your trouble?" asked Father.

"Heck, after whatcha did for my kid sister, you've paid in advance as far as I'm concerned. Next time, it'll be another matter."

26

"THE QUESTION, YOUR EMINENCE," said Father Baptist, "is just how much your chalice is worth to you."

We were back at the Chancery, standing in front of the trophy case in Cardinal Fulbright's private chapel. The sun was just going down and orange light was streaming in through the frosted windows.

"Explain yourself," said the cardinal, rubbing his purple bump furiously.

"It's like this, Your Eminence," said Father. "I have arranged to make contact with the man who I believe has your chalice. I realize you want him prosecuted, but I'm not in a position to do that—not if you want to recover your chalice. The police aren't in on this. I'm going through the underground and at considerable peril. It's a long story, and I'll gladly fill you in later, but right now moments are precious. I need to know how much you want that cup. Tell me what you're willing to pay for it."

The cardinal looked from Father to me. He bored into me with his deep-set eyes, came to a decision, and motioned for Father to come near. Cupping his hand, he whispered something into Father's ear.

Father's eyebrows went up a few notches. "Do you have that much on hand, Your Eminence?"

The cardinal whispered in his ear again.

"Well," said Father, "I suggest you order your clerks to get it together immediately."

The cardinal motioned for Monsignor Aspic, who was standing nearby jingling his change and rocking on his soles. Fulbright whispered orders into the monsignor's pink ear.

The monsignor's eyebrows did a few jumping jacks. He turned on his heels, tossed me a questioning look, and then shot off as though an exorcist was after him.

"May I ask," I asked as I maneuvered the Jeep out of the Chancery parking lot fifteen minutes later, "just how much the cardinal is willing to pay for his precious mug?"

Father held up the bulging envelope Morley Fulbright had thrust into his hands minutes before. The flap was sealed with wax. "That figure will remain his secret," he said at last, tucking the thing into the mysterious folds of his cassock. "But I think we can expect an archdiocese-wide fund drive some time soon. Perhaps a special collection for the poor."

"That much," I whistled.

"That much."

"So where shall we go," I asked, "to wait for Ernie's call?"

"We might as well go to Arthur's place," said Father. "After a day like today, it would be pleasant to put our minds on hold and enjoy the idle banter and pleasant companionship of a dinner party, especially an affair thrown by the Tumblars."

"Perhaps Arthur's sister will awaken long enough for us to actually meet her."

"That would be a pleasant surprise."

The night was going to be full of surprises. Some of them weren't all that pleasant.

27

"FATHER BAPTIST!" exclaimed the Bird of Paradise. "I would have been so disappointed if you hadn't made it."

"Which is precisely why I came," said Father, lightly pecking the back of her outstretched hand. "I try never to antagonize the press."

"Oh you," she said with a shake of her head, sending the strands of flowered appendages dangling from her fluorescent yellow hair into fluttering motion. "I'm not the press. I'm the *em*-press."

One thing I'll say for Kahlúa Hummingbird: she was a most *im*-pressive lady. She was an orchid garden, an exotic bird show, a semiprecious gem display, an old Tarzan movie, a Hawaiian luau, Ella Fitzgerald, and an African kalimba all rolled into one. She could stop a train with a swing of her hips, and ignite every cigar at a smokers' convention with a blink of her oyster-shell eyes.

"And Martin," she said, swishing her orbs and feathers my way, "you look simply dashing this evening."

If I had been drinking something other than ginger ale, I would have believed her. "Madam Hummingbird," I said, "it's always a pleasure."

"And the night is so young," she laughed, "and full of surprises."

Little did she know as she wandered away to dazzle the Tumblars one by one.

"Mr. Feeney," said a sweet, feminine voice. "I was so hoping that you'd be able to come this evening."

I turned to see Stella Billowack. Ever since she and Jonathan first laid eyes upon each other almost a month before, it was obvious where their relationship was headed. Pierre was already researching historical wedding ceremonies involving Knights and sabers. On the plus side she was smart, insightful, and very, very pretty. Her fulcra were right up there with the finest I've ever seen. On the minus side—and this was not her fault, of course—she was the offspring of Chief Montgomery Billowack, the slavering bulldog of a man who had given Father Baptist so much grief the last few months. The chief's main beef against Father Baptist was that Stella forsook her dad's Methodist roots and converted to the Catholic Faith, which proved to have even deeper roots in her. Father, true to his vocation and vows, had instructed Stella over her papa's huffing and puffing objections. Embracing the Truth, as far as I was concerned, was all that really mattered. Indeed, this singular fact put Stella so far on the plus side the minuses became inconsequential. Jonathan was a very lucky fellow.

"Stella," I said, kissing the back of her hand, "the pleasure is entirely mine. It's good to see you up and about since, um, you know—"

"I wouldn't be here at all," she said with a shiver, "if it weren't for you and Father Baptist." Self-consciously, her slender fingers went up to the tiny scars on her throat—the telltale sign of the danger to which she had nearly succumbed. "After all, I—"

Just then a door opened halfway and Arthur stepped into the small living room from the adjoining bedroom. "Ladies and gentlemen, Father Baptist and Mr. Feeney, may I present my sister, Beth."

A thin young woman with long black hair slipped shyly into the room as the Tumblars burst into enthusiastic applause. "Oh," she giggled, "please don't. I—I don't know what to say."

"Then say nothing, m'Lady," said Pierre, bowing deeply. His monocle slipped from its perch on his left cheek as he did so. It dangled from a black ribbon as he rose to his full height. "So lovely a guest of honor need make no speeches."

"And this," said Arthur, guiding his sister toward us, "is Father John Baptist and our good friend, Martin Feeney."

"Delighted," said Father.

"Ditto," said the gardener.

"Oh," said Beth. "Oh, Father Baptist, I'm so glad to meet you. I must apologize for ... you know, the way I ..."

"No apologies necessary," said Father. "You seem wide awake now."

"It won't last," she said, her eyes momentarily sad. "It never does. That's why Arthur is taking me to Italy."

"Dr. Zaiden has had remarkable success in cases like Beth's," said Arthur. "As soon as she's cured, she'll be back."

"Marvelous," smiled the gardener. "Beth, have you met Stella Billowack?"

"Why no," said Beth, taking Stella's hand the way ladies do. "Arthur has told me so much about you. Are you and Jonathan ...?"

"I think so," laughed Stella nervously. She had a charming way of rolling her eyes and biting her lower lip, then breaking out into a radiant smile. "That is, I hope so."

"I know so," winked Arthur. Then he turned to the others. "Listen, everyone. I suggest we proceed to the dining room."

"And how," said Edward, rubbing his hands together.

Arthur's apartment was small, but very old and proper, with all the appropriate rooms for a formal affair. The Tumblars, each in white tie and tails, led us through a wide arch into a room dominated by a large chandelier. Beneath the shimmering crystal umbrella lay a table set out with meticulous care. The silverware was mismatched but polished to a dazzling shine. The glasses were cheap but sparkling. And the platters of food ...

"Who cooked all this?" asked the gardener.

"Who do you think?" barked a familiar voice as the kitchen door burst open. Millie came stomping in holding a tureen of steaming onion soup. She paused to glare at Father and myself. "Well," her mouth snarled beneath twinkling eyes, "you didn't expect me to just sit at home and twiddle my thumbs, did you, just because you're too busy solving crimes to eat dinner?"

"Hurrah!" cheered the Tumblars.

"What about Monsignor Havermeyer?" asked the gardener.

"Out on a mission of mercy," said Millie. "Some priests still have it in them."

Father and I exchanged glances.

With a loud pop and a gush of foam, Pierre divvied up the champagne.

"Father," said Arthur as everyone found a chair to stand behind, "will you please lead us in saying Grace?"

"Of course," said Father. "In the name of the Father, and of the Son, and of the Holy Ghost. Amen."

"Bless us, O Lord," we all said together, "and these Thy gifts, which we are about to receive from Thy bounty, through Christ, Our Lord. Amen."

"May the Divine Assistance be always with us," said Father.

"And may the Souls of the Faithful Departed," said we all, "through the Mercy of God, rest in peace. Amen."

The final Sign of the Cross completed and the ladies seated, including Millie, we men rose to the task before us. It was quite a feast, and for a few brief moments, all was right with the world.

Beth stayed awake through dinner, but when the tapioca pudding was served she started blinking. Then her blinks turned into nods. I couldn't help but stare, fascinated. Right in the middle of an enlivened sentence her face would just go blank. Her eyes would flutter shut, her facial muscles would relax, and her jaw would sag slightly. Then, just as her head began to roll to one side, she'd snap wide awake, finishing her sentence.

As dessert progressed, these lapses came faster and faster until she was nodding off several times a minute.

"Oh dear," she said, realizing what was happening. "I'm afraid it's coming on again. Arthur, I think I'd better lie down."

"Of course," her brother said, instantly on his feet and at her side.

"If you'll all excuse me," she said, allowing herself to be led from the table.

We took that as a cue to get up and retire to the living room for brandy. In our host's absence, Pierre cleared his throat to propose the first toast.

"To Our Lady," he said, holding up his snifter. "Empress of All the Americas."

"To Our Lady," said the Tumblars, solemnly clinking their glasses.

"And to all my newfound friends," added Stella, including us all with a wide, slow wave of her arm.

"The pleasure is all ours, I assure you," beamed Jonathan.

"All his, he means," chided Edward.

"Well," said Jonathan, "mine, too."

"Especially yours," said Joel.

The room suddenly fell silent for a long second.

"All mine," said Jonathan, taking Stella's hand in his.

"Mmmmm-HM!" boomed Kahlúa Hummingbird.

"Hurrah!" cheered the Tumblars, patting Jonathan on the back and exchanging grand hugs with Stella.

In the midst of the din my attention was diverted by the sound of a door latch. I caught, as Arthur gingerly stepped out of the bedroom, a glimpse of Beth stretched out on top of the covers of a queen-size bed. She was lying on her back, her long hair carefully arranged on the pillow. Her hands were clasped on her tummy. She looked so peaceful—almost too peaceful. A shiver went through me as Arthur pulled the door closed behind him. The scene was a little too reminiscent of a "slumber room" at a funeral parlor.

"Martin?" asked Father.

"Hm?" I blinked.

"Where were you just now?"

"Oh, just thinking," I said. "I hope this doctor in Italy can help her. Did you see the way she kept drifting in and out?"

"You mean Beth," said Father. "Yes, it's hard to imagine what it would be like."

"I could use some fresh air. How about you?"

"Maybe for a minute or two. I really want to have a talk with Pierre while we're here."

We stepped through a sliding glass door onto a small balcony. Behind us, the Tumblars were taking turns toasting their favorite Saints, and maybe a few they didn't know much about. It was a great way to make the brandy flow.

"To Saint Ambrose," said Joel.

"To Saint Ambrose," they cheered. Clinks and slurps.

"To Saint Maximilian Kolbe." Cheers, clinks, and slurps.

"To Saint Athanasia ... To Saint Tarsicius ... To Saint Agnes of Montepulciano ... To Saint Maurice and the Theban Legion ... To Saint Ursula with her 11,010 Companions ..."

Father and I stood on the balcony, watching cars roll by on the street below.

"You're worried about Pierre?" I asked presently.

"When we arrived," said Father, "I asked him if the police had questioned him today. He became evasive—said he was out on an assignment when they phoned the office. When he got back to the *Artsy* he was in a hurry to come over here to help Arthur prepare for this evening."

"You mean he didn't return Taper's call?"

"Apparently not—and that bothers me."

"Well, after all, it's Pierre Bontemps we're talking about, not Ernie Corben."

"Some men," Pierre was announcing, "are born to have a good time. Other men strive to have a good time. Still other men have a good time thrust upon them." As he said this, several of the Tumblars were holding up fingers to show how many times they'd heard this before.

"And you?" cooed Kahlúa Hummingbird.

At the sound of her question, I turned to observe. Lady Hummingbird had her arm around Madam Millie's shoulder, and both ladies were sporting glasses brimming with dark liquid. It wasn't often I got to see Millie having a good time. I was happy for her.

"Me," said Pierre, taking up his monocle to fog it with his breath. "Me—" He seemed distracted for a moment. Something about his monocle caught his attention. He looked closely at it, then shrugged, dropping it so that it dangled at the end of its black ribbon. "Where was I? Oh yes. Me, I simply *have* a good time. It's my name, you see. Bontemps."

"Goooood times," chanted the Tumblars. "Good times, good times—"

Just then the doorbell rang.

The banter subsided as Arthur strode out of my line of sight to answer it.

"Nonetheless," Father was saying beside me, "I've got a bad feeling."

"Well don't look now," I said. "But here comes—"

"Lieutenant Taper!" greeted Jonathan.

"Sergeant Wickes!" chimed Edward.

"What brings you here?" asked Arthur and Joel.

"Here it comes," said Father, walking back through the sliding glass doorway into the living room.

I hesitated for a moment. I don't know why—well, yes I do. Something was tugging at the periphery of my vision. To my left was a curtained window. I judged that it belonged to the bedroom into which Arthur had taken his sister to lie down. Just then a puff of wind fluttered the curtain, and I saw Beth's silhouette. She was sitting in a chair. At first I thought she was looking down upon the cars going by on the asphalt below. Then I realized her head was bowed forward in sleep. Apparently she'd roused herself from the bed only to fall asleep again in the chair.

As the curtain fell back into place, I took a deep breath and followed Father Baptist into the living room.

"I'm sorry to intrude on your revelry," Taper was saying, "but this is official business."

"What do you mean, 'official'?" asked Arthur.

"We've been trying to contact you all day, Pierre," said Wickes. "You didn't return our calls."

"Well," said Pierre, "I was out on assignment—"

"I can vouch for that, Officers," said Madam Hummingbird.

"Okay," said Taper, his voice sharp with irritation. "We'll let that go for now. But Pierre, I have to ask you this: where were you Saturday night around nine forty-five?"

"Why," said Pierre, "I was with my friends here, celebrating the arrival of Arthur's dear sister, Beth."

"You all agree with that?" asked Taper.

"Certainly," they said severally. "Of course. Sure."

"I don't think so," said Taper sternly. "I think you're all lying."

The Tumblars ruffled their tailcoats in indignation.

I noticed Taper noticing Stella Billowack for the first time with a start. After all, she was his boss's daughter and he had just included her in his accusation, even though she hadn't been involved on the night in question. Millie and Kahlúa were both standing with hands on hips, equally insulted, ready for a brawl.

"See here, Lieutenant," said Edward. "You've got no business coming here and—"

"I said this is official," said Taper, "and I meant it. Father Baptist's visit to the home of Mr. Roderick Roundhead earlier today stirred a hornet's nest of activity."

All Tumblar eyes turned to Father, startled.

"Did you say Roundhead?" asked Arthur.

"Isn't that—?" coughed Jonathan. "You mean—?"

"The same," said Father.

"A man of considerable influence," said Taper. "When he learned of the theft of Saint Valeria, he called the police commissioner and the mayor demanding a complete and comprehensive investigation. Detectives in both Homicide and Burglary were shifted onto the case. In addition, Mr. Roundhead ordered private detectives in his employ into the field, and they've been phoning in reports all day."

Pierre stood his ground, chin out, shoulders back—but I'm sure I caught the glimmer of uncertainty in his eyes.

"We now know," continued Taper, "that Pierre was not with the rest of you—certainly not at 9:45. At that time he was at LAX, specifically the air freight dock at the south terminal, arranging for the shipment of a large crate. The clerks remember a man in a tailcoat, and so do the workmen who hoisted the crate out of the back of the van he was driving. One of them remembered the dented fender, which means the van probably belonged to Edward. We have a copy of the receipt which records the time at 9:47."

"What are you saying?" asked Madam Hummingbird. "What are you accusing Pierre of doing?"

"Pierre," said Taper, pointing. "Is that the monocle you were wearing on Saturday?"

Pierre gripped the circlet at the end of its ribbon. "I only have the one, Lieutenant."

"Let me see it."

Shrugging, Pierre held it out on his outstretched hand.

"How long has the lens been missing?" asked Wickes.

"There you have me, Officers," said Pierre. "I only just noticed that the lens was gone a moment ago. I'm sure it was intact Saturday morning when we were all at the mausoleum—"

"Saturday morning?" asked Wickes.

"Yes."

"And what about Saturday evening?"

"I don't know what you mean."

"Pierre," said Taper, "we found the lens in the mausoleum. Its purpose eluded us at first, because it's just a flat, round piece of glass—not a prescription lens. You just wear the monocle for effect, don't you?"

"That's what they're for, Lieutenant," said Pierre.

"The lens we found had been stepped on, broken, and it was on the floor next to the body of Roger Galloway, the guard who was found murdered. Do you deny that you were there at the mausoleum Saturday night?"

"Don't say anything," said Joel.

"We can fix the time of the murder at nine o'clock," said Wickes.

"We've found splinters and nails on the asphalt drive near the entrance to the mausoleum," said Taper. "We think that you and some friends—" He looked around the room with an accusatory glare. "—removed the coffin of Saint Valeria from the crypt and crated it right there in the cemetery. We know you couldn't have done it alone, Pierre. Your accomplices helped you put the crate into the back of the van. Why you were stealing the body of a Saint, I don't know. What I do know is that you went back into the mausoleum, probably alone, perhaps to cement the facing stone back into place—that was certainly doable by one person. Your accomplices went off to establish alibis. I think Galloway, the guard, surprised you in the dark. Perhaps you panicked. You knocked him dead with the facing stone."

"Now see here—" said Edward.

"No," said Taper, "you listen to me: all of you. If you participated in the theft of the body, and a homicide was committed during the commission of that crime, then you are all accessories to murder."

Well, that put a damper on things.

Kahlúa let go of Millie and gripped Pierre's arm. Stella was holding onto Jonathan for dear life. I planted my cane firmly between my feet and braced myself for the worst. Father Baptist sighed, closed his eyes, and whispered a prayer to Saint Anthony of Padua.

"Pierre," said Taper after several long seconds, "do you have anything to say?"

Pierre straightened himself to his full height. "There is nothing I can tell you, Lieutenant, about the events of Saturday evening."

"So what happens now?" asked Father Baptist.

"We're taking Pierre with us for further questioning," said Wickes, trying his best to sound detached and official. The quaver in his voice belayed his discomfiture. "The rest of you are free at present, but you are not to leave the city."

"If you're taking Pierre to headquarters," said Jonathan, "we're coming with you."

"Perhaps that would save time," said Taper. "Pierre will come in our car. The rest of you can follow in your respective vehicles. All except you, Edward. We're impounding your van to check it for fingerprints and other evidence."

Edward took that bit of news with a stern curl of his shoulders. "Very well, I'll come with Arthur."

"I'd better stay here," said Arthur. "Beth can't be left alone."

"I can remain with her," offered Millie.

"No, thank-you," said Arthur.

"Well, at least I can stay and clean up."

"That would be most appreciated," he said a mite sternly, "but I'd prefer that you don't." With that, Arthur turned and went into the bedroom to check on his sister.

It wasn't often that someone spoke that way to our dear Millie. Cheeks imploded and eyes bulging, she got herself under control and went to fetch her wrap.

"Don't you worry, Dear," Kahlúa called after our outraged housekeeper. "I'll drive you home. You, too, Stella, Honey"

"I want to stay with Jonathan," said the chief's daughter.

"No," said Jonathan, visibly shaken, "you'd better go with Millie and Kahlúa. I have to deal with this."

"Just wait'll I tell Daddy," said Stella, releasing his arm.

"He already knows, Stell," said Wickes. "He sent us here."

Taper walked over to Father Baptist. "I'm sorry, Jack. The evidence just piled up so quickly, and I didn't know where to reach you."

"Well," said Miss Hummingbird, feathers and flowers waving. "This will get quite a write-up in the *Artsy*. I'll want an exclusive, Father, when you clear Pierre of all charges."

"You're confident that I'll do that," said Father Baptist.

"Of course," she said. "He's Pierre Bontemps, after all. He's many things, and foremost among them, he's innocent."

"Will you be coming?" asked Taper to Father.

"Yes."

"Good. And you'd better call your lawyer friend—"

"Drew de Montfort."

"—yes, because Pierre is going to need an attorney before the night's over. And they all might need counsel before noon tomorrow."

"You're wrong about Pierre," said Father. "You know it and I know it. And you're still off base about the murder of Roger Galloway."

"I wish I were," said Taper. "You know I'm fond of Pierre—all these guys—but the evidence is all but conclusive."

I detached myself and headed for the bathroom, thinking I might not get the chance to use a clean one for some time. Arthur was just coming back into the living room, pulling the bedroom door closed behind him. I caught another glimpse of Beth, back on the bed as before, her hair spread out on the pillow and her hands clasped over her stomach. Apparently her stint at the window had been short-lived. Imagine: a narcoleptic having trouble sleeping.

"Is she all right?" I asked in a whisper.

"As good as she gets," said Arthur. He grabbed my arm. "Martin, you and Father have got to get Pierre out of this. Pierre didn't—couldn't—kill anyone."

"You're preaching to the choir here," I said. "But something's not right. Pierre's hiding something, and if you know what it is, you'd better tell Father Baptist."

"I can't tell him anything," said Arthur.

"Can't or won't?"

Arthur just looked at me, released my arm, and walked away.

28

"SPEAK TO ME, PIERRE!" roared Father Baptist, pounding his fist on the coffee-stained table in the interrogation room at Police Headquarters. "They've traced your movements to LAX. You did ship a crate on TWA flight 952. It departed on schedule just after midnight. The clerks remember you, likewise the loading crew, and the police found a copy of the shipping receipt in your apartment. Now what do you have to say to all that?"

Pierre was seated across from him. His white tie was drooping somewhat, but otherwise he look composed and determined.

"I have nothing to say," said Mr. Bontemps.

"You realize," said Father, "that they've traced that crate through Heathrow in London, then to Paris, then on to Rome. You see? Mr. Roundhead's private hounds have already hacked their way into the airline's computer—illegal, perhaps, but effective just the same. The information can be verified through regular channels later. They've sent operatives by chartered jet to catch up with the crate in Rome. They'll find it, and they'll open it, and—"

Pierre swallowed.

The gardener, propped in the corner, was tracing patterns on the linoleum floor with the tip of his cane, slaughtering himself at tic-tac-toe. Seeing Pierre in this awful place was ruining my concentration.

Father Baptist leaned back in the rickety chair. He closed his eyes. Then he opened them again. "Wait a minute. You couldn't just send a coffin through customs, certainly not containing human remains, not without all kinds of paperwork—Health Department certification, proof of ownership, kinship, whatever. You may have connections through the *Artsy,* but you don't have *those* kinds of connections. So what's going on? You sent an empty coffin? Perhaps an empty crate? What for?"

"I can't tell you that," said Pierre.

"Then what can you tell me?"

"Nothing."

"This is serious, Pierre."

"I know, Father."

"They're accusing you of murder."

"I don't know anything about that."

"Were you there at the mausoleum when Galloway was killed?"

"I'm not going to tell you anything about anything that happened Saturday night, Father. You're just going to have to trust me on this."

"Trust you?" Father leaned forward, gripping the edge of the table. "Trust you regarding what? You're right in the middle of a murder charge, and—"

Father stopped suddenly, then got up from his chair. "Wait another minute. You haven't been charged yet. Why not? Because they know whoever took Saint Valeria's coffin couldn't have done it alone. The other Tumblars all have alibis—like their timely visit to the rectory—so the police haven't yet figured out how you maneuvered the coffin. That's the weak link in their case. There's still time; maybe I can help you yet. Now, will you tell me: were you involved in the theft of Saint Vale-ria?"

"No," said Pierre.

"No, you're not involved?"

"No, I won't tell you."

Father looked at Pierre, then at me.

We left.

Just as we were stepping outside into the evening air, there was a swish of cloth and a clatter of heels, and suddenly Sybil Wexler was beside us.

And get this: she was wearing *red* again.

"Father Baptist," she hiss-whispered, looking around anxiously, "I'm going to tell you something, and I'm telling you because I want you to know that I'm not like Tragg Holcomb. I'm sorry I got stuck with him for a partner. He's acting like a creep, and I have to get along with him somehow. I think his dad was an apostate Catholic who turned televangelist or something. Small-time, odd cable channels, anti-Catholic literature—that sort of thing. Daddy was the black sheep of his family, and Tragg is his father's son. That's what I heard, anyway. So how do you out black-sheep your own father?"

"You become a son-of-a-sheep?" asked the gardener.

She gave me an odd look, then slipped a sheet of paper out of her red purse and handed it to Father. "I've been doing some follow-up—you know, phoning the pawnshops that were burglarized to see if they've had any further trouble, that sort of thing. And guess what?"

"Let me think," said Father, running his eyes down the page. "Every shop owner on this list received an envelope postmarked in Van Nuys, an envelope filled with cash, cash in the precise amount they were asking for the objects in the first place plus something to cover their damages."

"You *are* good," said Sybil. "If the theft of your cardinal's chalices is connected with this case, then he's due to receive a large, bulging envelope in the mail one of these days."

"That," said Father, fingering something under the folds of his cassock, "should prove interesting. Tell me, Sybil, has Roring said anything useful yet?"

"Not to us," she answered. "He's clammed up. Your friend, Monsignor Havermeyer, went to see him about an hour ago. The monsignor insisted on privacy so I don't know what passed between them."

"Perhaps the monsignor heard Roring's confession," I suggested.

"Could be," said Sybil. Gosh, she looked good in red. "The floor nurse told us that Roring seemed to calm down after Havermeyer left."

"How about Willie?" I asked.

She shrugged. "He's still unconscious."

"Find anything at his shop?"

"Nothing we could make heads or tails of."

"In other words," said Father, "nothing you could pin on him."

"I already apologized," said Sybil.

"True," said Father. "But I'd still like to know whether you were watching him or tailing us."

"Well, we weren't tailing you."

"So what aroused your suspicions about him?"

"I can't tell you that," she said defensively.

"Ah," said Father, "the police must protect their sources."

"Oh," said the gardener, "an anonymous tip."

"Look," said Sybil, "I'm trying to be fair with you—"

Something chirped with electronic insistence inside Father's cassock. He looked down at himself, unfamiliar with the phenomenon.

"That sounds like a cell phone," said Sybil.

"Of course," said Father, digging around for it. It was chirping a second time when he produced it, groped for the "send" button, and held it up to his ear. "Father Baptist," he said awkwardly.

"It would seem," said Sybil while we waited, "that your Father Baptist has taken a flying leap into the twenty-first century."

"Better late," I said. "But best not at all."

She looked at me without comprehension.

I smiled.

"Got it," said Father. "We'll be right there."

He fumbled around with the thing and finally got it tucked away again.

"Something important?" asked Sybil.

"Something profoundly important," said Father. "You'll excuse us, Sybil. Martin and I must keep an appointment."

"You seem to stir up trouble everywhere you go," observed Sybil.

"Or," I countered, "trouble follows us. Hard to say."

"Whatever," said Father. "Good night, Sybil. And thanks for the information."

"Good night, Father, Martin."

Father and I strode quickly to the Jeep—he in the lead, of course, me struggling behind.

"Now there's a bit of irony for you," I said as I turned the car out into the whizzing evening traffic.

"Which irony is that?" asked Father.

"Well," I said, "Morley lays down a heap of cash for his precious Murkenmug, only to get his money back in short order. Don't tell me there's justice in the world."

"I'll admit that sometimes it's rare. In this case, we'll just have to wait and see."

"Shouldn't we maybe postpone this trip into the underworld?"

"Why? You don't trust Ernie?"

"Of course not. Do you?"

"Of course not."

"Well, that's settled, but it's beside the point, Father. Where you go, I go. I ain't much of a sidekick as Tontos go, but I'm like glue—all gooey and hard to wash off."

"Martin."

"Yes, Father."

"Will you please get to the point?"

"The point? Sure: how can you leave Pierre at a time like this?"

"I'm not abandoning him."

"You're sure not staying with him."

"What good would that do? He's not helping himself, and he sure isn't helping me. He's got the Tumblars for moral support, if that's what he wants. What he *needs* is entirely different, and I'm not sure I'm in a position to provide that—at least, not yet."

I chewed my lower lip thoughtfully for a while, turning Father's words over in my mind. I shut off the mental rotisserie, however, as "Ernie's 'World Famous' Hotdogs" came into view.

29

"OKAY, THIS IS IT," SAID ERNIE. He was hunched in the back of our Jeep with his spindly elbows hooked on our headrests. He'd been barking a complicated series of directions for the last twenty minutes. I was completely lost, and he had really, really, really bad breath.

"This?" asked Father, gazing up at the shattered ruin of an abandoned hotel as I pulled to a stop at the curb. It was a ghastly-looking place, a crumbling wreck of a once-pretentious lodge for the well-to-do which had gone the way of the city dump.

"You expected the 'Polo Lounge'?" asked Ernie.

"I don't know what I expected," said Father. "This sort of thing is new to us."

"Well, you'll soon get the hang of it," said Ernie. "Now listen: you two go in through the front door, cross the lobby, and follow the hallway that leads to the back of the joint. There's a service elevator there. Press the button marked 'P.' It'll take you down to what yoosta be an underground parkin' lot until the city engineers condemned the place after the Northridge quake. Down there you'll meet some guy."

"Some guy?" I asked. "Just some guy?"

"Right," said Ernie. "He's expectin' you. You convince him you're legit and you're in. If you don't—well, just convince him."

"Is it safe to leave the car here?" I asked, throwing open my door and struggling outside.

"Safe as any place in this town," shrugged Ernie, already standing on the sidewalk.

"And what about you?" asked Father of the hotdog king.

Ernie laughed. "I know my way home. Don't worry 'bout me. You watch out for yourselves. I'll tell you this: someone down the chute is very interested in you two. When I started makin' calls, I could tell I was raisin' eyebrows. I don't like that. But, I owed you one, Father. This is the payoff. Good luck to you."

"You might pray a Hail Mary for us," I suggested.

"Hah," chortled our departing guide. "I might at that."

With that, Ernie took off down the street. I watched him turn at the first corner and disappear behind an angled wooden fence.

"Whoops," said Father. "I forgot to give him his cell phone."

"Something tells me he's got more where that came from," I said. "Don't worry, Father. If we survive, you can always return it. If we don't you can call him from Purgatory."

"Well," said Father, ascending the stairs to the front door, "no use putting this off. You've got the reliquary?"

"Yup."

"Then let's put our lives under Mary's protection, and trust in God."

"Okay, Father, we're in the best of hands."

As we crossed the deserted lobby, passing the counter where the desk clerk once clicked his heels and twirled his moustache, Father added, "And don't forget the words of Pope Pius IX: 'Place on thy heart one drop of the Precious Blood of Jesus and fear nothing.'"

"Imagining the first part is always easy," said the gardener as they walked down the forbidding hallway, "but mustering the second is another thing."

"But," said Father, stabbing the button marked "P," "the former, if prayed in earnest, will produce the latter."

"Eventually," we said together as the door rattled closed.

The interchange was rehearsed, you see. This wasn't the first time Martin Feeney was scared out of his wits.

It was a long way down—or at least, it certainly took a long time. Perhaps the contraption was simply so rusty it couldn't fall any faster. What am I saying?

Anyway, we did arrive in the subterranean parking lot. It was echoey, dark, cold, and smelled of stale garbage—just the sort of place where you're likely to meet "some guy" who's a pal of Ernie Corben of hotdog fame.

"Okay," said a voice out the darkness. "Which one of you is the priest?"

"I am," said Father, peering into the smelly nothingness.

"I don't trust priests," said the voice.

"Neither does he," ventured the gardener.

A shape materialized out of the gloom. He was a big, big man. He reached up and pulled a string. A single bare bulb flickered to life, revealing a ceiling of caked seepage and a floor of sour splatter.

"I'm Some Guy," he said.

No kidding. That's what he said. That's who he said he was.

"I'm Father Baptist."

"I'm M-m-martin Feeney."

"I see your collar now," said the guy known as Some Guy to Father. Then he repeated, "I don't trust priests."

"You should see the sign on the doorway to Father's study," I found myself saying. I don't know what possessed me to open my trap just then, seeing as how I'm woodwork around the borders of most scenes in this story. The gearshift knob inside my head suddenly slipped from neutral to second. I was as surprised as everyone at each word that came out of my mouth.

"A sign?" asked the big man.

"A quote by Saint John Eudes," said the quivering gardener.

"What quote?" asked Some Guy.

"You'd like it," I said, visualizing the hand-drawn message hung from a nail on the frame of the door. You can't miss it. I'm surprised that Tragg didn't hit on it. Well, come to think of it, most people say nothing about it—like it's a great secret we're all keeping from Father. Right, sure.

Anyway, as I was saying, I could see it so clearly in my mind's eye that I was reading the words rather than summoning them from memory. It wasn't until I was halfway through my recitation that it dawned on me what a horrible risk I was taking. Me and my mouth. Oh well, once the ol' cranial gearshift was engaged, there was no holding back:

> The most evident mark of God's anger, and the most terrible castigation He can inflict upon the world, is manifest when He permits His people to fall into the hands of a clergy who are more in name than in deed, priests who practice the cruelty of ravening wolves rather than the charity and affection of devoted shepherds ...

"Say," said Mr. Guy, "I kinda like that."

"Good," said I. "Then you'll like the next part:

> ... They abandon the things of God to devote themselves to the things of the world and, in their saintly calling of holiness, they spend their time in profane and worldly pursuits. When God permits such things, it is a very positive proof that He is thoroughly angry with His people, and is visiting His most dreadful wrath upon them.

"Wow," said Some Guy, smiling as though he was listening to his favorite song, "you just maybe got something there."

"Could be," I agreed with him.

He stepped closer to me. "I kinda like you."

Oooooooh great, thought the gardener.

"This priest," he said, indicating Father Baptist with a nod of his enlarged forehead, "him I still don't trust."

"You'd trust Martin over me?" asked Father, surprised. Surprised? Why was he so surprised?

"You'd trust me over him?" asked the gardener, equally surprised, if not more.

"You I like," said Some Guy. "Him, I don't trust."

"Okay, Martin," said Father, turning to me. "You pitch the deal."

"Me? But I don't even know what you're—"

"Go ahead. Rely on your instincts."

"See?" said Some Guy. "That's why I don't trust you, Padre." The matter clarified as far as he was concerned, he turned to me. "Like he said, you do the talkin'."

"Martin," said Father. "In the name of Heaven, proceed."

"Um," I said, not wanting to encourage Some Guy to like me too much, and not having a clue as to Father Baptist's plan.

Slowly, I reached into my pocket and pulled out the reliquary. "Well, you see, it's this way. I have here—"

"I know, I know," said Some Guy. "Some relic you wanna sell. Ernie called ahead. So how much you want for it?"

Now that stopped me cold. I certainly couldn't put a price on a chip from the Crown of Thorns, and even if I could, I had no intention of selling it.

"Martin," said Father.

"Ahem," I coughed, then mentally flung myself off a cliff. "B-b-before I tell you, Mr. Guy, I need to know if what I have here will stop with you, or will you just pass it on to someone else?"

"Eh?" asked Some Guy. "What's that?"

"In other words," I said, "are you the one who's got the word out around the city that you—you personally—want relics?"

"Me?" asked Some Guy, dumbfounded. "You're askin' me? What are you tryin' to pull? Well, what the heck. There's only two of you. From here on, you're covered. You cross me, you're dead."

"I d-d-don't want to cross you," I gulped, not at all following his train of thought. "I just want to know if you're the ultimate buyer, the last guy, the hook on the end of the chain—in other words, are you the guy who *really* wants this?"

"So what if I'm not?"

I took a deep breath. "Then I'm going to ask you to pass us on, as it were, to the next man—the man you would pass it on to. He's the man I need to see. You see, Mr. Guy, this relic is very important to me. It's the dearest thing I have in this world. But things have taken a turn, and I need help—and I need it now. It's not important why, let's call it a tough break. But my situation is urgent enough for me to resort to trying to sell this relic. I don't expect you—I don't expect anyone—to understand. I just want to meet the man who wants this treasure, who really *wants* it, so I can ascertain if his intentions are honorable. If they are, so much the good. If not, I may just change my mind."

Some Guy took another step closer. "You're nuts—you know that? But I still like you."

Father Baptist, who had been tense up to that point, seemed to relax.

"I'm gonna take a chance on you," beamed Mr. Guy. "I'm gonna do it because not only do I think you're funny, but because I have a hunch the guy at the end of the line would appreciate your position. I shouldn't tell you this, and I shouldn't do it, but I'm gonna arrange for you to meet him."

"Y-y-you are?" I squeaked.

"I still don't trust him," he said, nodding again toward Father Baptist. "And by the way: if you guys are cops, or if you're wired, you won't get anywhere near him anyway."

"Y-y-y-you mean you'd kill us?"

"I mean," said Some Guy, "that from this point on, it's high security."

30

YOU'RE NOT GOING TO BELIEVE THIS. I swear it's the truth, but even Monsignor Havermeyer was skeptical when I told him what happened next.

First, Some Guy led us through the dingy parking level to a metal detector, just like at an airport. We had to step through this doorway, and each time it beeped we had to discard whatever made it do so. The cell phone caused a squawk, and when Father explained that it was Ernie's, Some Guy took it and shoved it deep inside his own coat. My keys caused a howl, and I certainly didn't like seeing them disappear into Mr. Guy's change pocket.

"Don't get upset, Little Fella," said Some Guy. "You'll get all your stuff back before the night is over. I needed to get everythin' metal off of you before you go through that."

"That?" I asked.

He pointed to another freestanding doorframe that loomed ahead in the gloom. This one was more complicated. In fact, it looked sinister. I didn't know its purpose or function. I figured it probably shot people with enough froo-froo rays to keep them glowing at night for years to come.

"Don't worry," said Some Guy. "It's some sorta magnetic thingamajigger—don't ask me. But if you're wearin' so much as a tie clip you might find yourself hangin' by it from the ceilin'."

A pleasant thought.

Father and I each stepped from the north to the south pole and returned.

"Okay," said Some Guy, handing us back our things as he stared intently at a video screen. "Neither of you swallowed a bomb."

"How would I set it off if I did?" asked the gardener.

"You could've wired it to your belly button," said Mr. Guy. No kidding, that's what he said.

"What now?" asked Father.

"Impatient, ain'tcha?" sneered Some Guy. "Another reason why I don't trust priests. Well, you just come over here 'round this ol' boiler, and you'll see what's next."

Just around the ol' boiler was nothing less than a stretch limousine. This was no secondhand hearse with a rewelded chassis and a rebuilt engine. This was a long, lithe, deeply waxed, regularly vacuumed, oh-so-plush cocktail parlor on wheels.

"Inside," said Some Guy, donning a chauffeur's cap two sizes too small. "You're goin' for a ride."

So there we were, seated in the back of this luxury sedan complete with full bar, curtains front and back, and side windows tinted jet black. The bar was not stocked with Saint Thomas, though. No class whatsoever.

"Father," I said, as Some Guy made a flurry of useless, confusing changes of direction.

"Yes, Martin."

"You said you haven't abandoned Pierre."

"That's right."

"So he's in that horrid room with nothing to drink but twice-through coffee. We're making great progress here as we zigzag around town in the longest possible distance between two straight lines. Perhaps we are on the trail of the cardinal's Murkencup, but we're not even positive of that. What I don't see is how this is helping Pierre."

"That's what he said, sir ..." came Mr. Guy's voice through the front curtain, apparently communicating with his boss via car phone. "... That's right ... to change his mind, sir ..."

"Think, Martin," said Father. "The man we seek knew enough about what he was after to steal—or, more likely, to cause to be stolen—four reliquaries from the cardinal's trophy case. Four great Doctors of the Universal Church. He also procured two chalices, one of great historical value and the other a self-aggrandizing bauble. Surely he knew the difference. Yet when the opportunity presented itself, he seized both. What can we surmise from that?"

"That the reliquaries and 'next to' chalice were for himself, and the Murkenmug was for revenge? He has it in for Cardinal Fulbright—a grudge of some kind?"

"Excellent, Martin. Now, consider further: the man we seek has caused religious items to be stolen from pawnshops, but he turns around and pays the shopkeepers for their losses and damages."

"He has a peculiar juxtaposition of moral predilections."

"Well put," said Father. "You want to know how finding this man will help Pierre. Reflect on this: the man who would desire to possess the 'next to the Grail' *and* would let someone like you approach him with a relic while stipulating that you might change your mind if you find him dishonorable—would not this be the sort of man who would go to great lengths to obtain the relics of Saint Valeria, her body having just been consigned to an unmarked tomb?"

"I begin to see your point, Father."

"This man is moved by righteous indignation, perhaps, as well as greed."

"You think he's a Roman Catholic?"

"I think that's obvious from the nature of the objects he desires. So you see, Martin, if I can find this man, and place him or his accomplices at the time and place of the death of Roger Galloway, Pierre would be off the hook. So I repeat: I am not abandoning Pierre."

"Well, when you put it that way—"

"You guys sure do talk in weird circles," called Some Guy over his shoulder through the curtain.

"Nothing like the ones you're driving in," ulped the gardener.

"So you're listening," said Father.

"Of course," said Mr. Guy, "'cause I don't trust you."

"How do we know," asked the gardener, "that you're not taking us to some abandoned warehouse to shoot us?"

"The thought had crossed my mind," nodded Some Guy. "One of you, anyway. But don't worry, we're almost there."

The limo slowed.

"Father," I said.

Father Baptist touched his finger to his lips. He was listening intently.

I perked up my ears, but the ol' lobes didn't register anything.

The limo almost stopped, but then rolled on a ways, then slowed again, then took a sudden but smooth nose-dive, sending my stomach into orbit. Funny how that works. Then we leveled off, slowed, and finally came to a complete stop.

"Fourth floor," said Some Guy, tipping his hat. "Ladies' Lingerie, Bath Towels, Religious Stuff, and Cement Overshoes."

That Some Guy, he's such a cut-up.

31

"WHAT A WONDERFUL SELECTION YOU HAVE," said the gardener as he and Father Baptist emerged from the limousine. We found ourselves parked in a large, bare, well-lit place—all cement surfaces and round pillars supporting a low ceiling. "Which way, did you say, to the lingerie?"

"That way," said Some Guy, indicating a doorway. "I stay here."

"Thank-you," said Father.

"Anytime, Padre." Mr. Guy cupped his hand at the side of his mouth. "But I'll never trust any of you priests."

"I commend you," smiled Father, "and thank-you all the more."

I saluted Mr. Guy with my cane and followed Father through the doorway, which led down a plain concrete corridor.

"I don't know what your plan is, Father," I whispered. "But I strongly advise that you don't tick off the man at the end of this hallway."

"And why do you say that, Martin?"

"Because if he's rich enough to afford all this, he's influential enough to make us disappear. The Cement Overshoes Department is just back there a ways, and they're running a sale on anchor chains."

"A salient point about wealth and influence. I'll keep it in mind when negotiations commence."

"What negotiations are those, Father?"

"Well, as you suggest, I may be parlaying for our lives."

"Ah yes, I was afraid that was what you meant."

"Chin up, Martin. I don't really think we're in bodily danger. I'm beginning to think that this might be more a matter of conscience, perhaps of the very soul. Prayers would do ... no ... harm ..."

His voice trailed off as we came to a pair of swinging maple doors. Having pushed through, we found ourselves in a room that could have passed for the office of a high-priced attorney. It was dominated by a large, glass-covered desk, and behind the desk in a high-backed leather swivel chair sat the man who was the goal of our quest. He was wearing a very fine tuxedo, the kind of outfit that would send the Tumblars into swoons of ecstasy.

"Ah, Father Baptist, Mr. Feeney," he said, plucking a smoldering cigar from his mouth as he rose to greet us.

"Mr. Roderick Roundhead," said Father.

The gardener said nothing—nor could he have, since he had lost his tongue somewhere between Women's Lingerie and Religious Stuff.

"Please," said our host, motioning us to two comfortable leather chairs across from him.

As we settled into our seats, Mr. Roundhead made a grand gesture of pausing in half-sit to flick the ash from his cigar into a ponderous ashtray. Said receptacle was none other than Cardinal Morley Fulbright's precious Murkenstein Chalice, all sparkling and polished on the outside, but a sink of sour ashes within. I'd only seen the photo in the brochure, but I'd know that ugly mug anywhere. As far as I was concerned, the cigar ash was a nice touch.

I looked at Father and saw that he recognized it, too.

"Ahem," said Mr. Roundhead officiously. "At last the reason for your visit to my home this afternoon becomes clear. You were 'scoping me out' to see if I'm connected to the wave of thefts involving holy objects. Not very subtle, Father. *'Le San Pres'que Grall,'* indeed. Do you take me for a fool?"

"I'll readily admit that I underestimated you," said Father. He waved at our surroundings and shrugged. "A mistake, I assure you, I won't repeat."

"Hrmph," hrmphed Mr. Roundhead, striking a match and re-lighting his cigar, rolling the Cuban log in his ring-studded fingers. "And now you come to me here, like a peddler in the night, with something for sale. The question presents itself: are you actually here to sell Mr. Feeney's relic, or are you here to apprehend me? Rest assured that I don't intend to underestimate you, either."

"So," said Father.

"So tell me," said Mr. Roundhead, "what you want."

"And you would trust me to tell you the truth?"

Mr. Roundhead's green eyes flickered. "I would say that the time for child's play and hide-and-seek is past. You're under my roof now, and as the guests of a proper host you have my protection for the moment. But you are here, and that itself provides us with a dilemma. I'll remind you that guests are under certain obligations, too."

"I am aware of that," said Father. "So tell me, what do you think I want from you?"

"Well, now that you've found me, an explanation, for one thing." With a flourish, Roundhead tossed another barrel of ash into the Murkenmug. "You see this wretched cup about which the cardinal so concerns himself? Therein lies the tale, Father. The microcosm reflects the macrocosm. Here, in small, we see the layout of the big problem."

"Indeed," said Father. "Tell me more."

"Our beloved cardinal whines and shrieks over the theft of this ugly keepsake, while he sells off priceless artifacts of our Faith to balance his books! Which, I ask you, is the greater crime? I see churches everywhere gutted of these beautiful things. Pastors, who should be diligent keepers of such treasures, sell them to vendors who have no idea of their history or spiritual significance. The shopkeepers sell them to people who appreciate them even less. Old Catholic families like mine look on in horror as these offenses go unchecked—did I say unchecked?—indeed, these offenses are *encouraged* by our very shepherds. We see these wonderful symbols of our sublime Catholic Faith tossed out like garbage by the very men who should be using them as well as preserving them for future generations." He seemed to catch himself. "Well, I won't take up your time with speeches."

"My time is yours," said Father, "and I don't mind speeches of this sort."

"I'll tell you a secret, Father," said Mr. Roundhead, tossing the stump of his cigar into the Murkencup. He leaned forward on his elbows and rubbed his palms together. "Ten years ago in a place I will not reveal, I happened upon a bishop who will remain nameless in a bar. You'll appreciate my evasiveness in a moment. I recognized this man who had found a hole to crawl into where no one else did. We talked long into the night. He was suffering from a guilty conscience. He was tormented by the realization that he had abandoned the beliefs of his youth for the sake of ecclesiastical power. Worst of all, he knew he didn't have the guts to set things right. Long story short, at dawn the next morning, he imparted a great gift upon me."

"Oh?" said Father.

"You no doubt know that a bishop has the power of bestowing Knighthood. At six o'clock that morning, with a sword retrieved from a suit of armor in his residence, he performed the ritual. I became a Knight, Sir Roderick Roundhead, and I swore that morning I would do everything in my power to protect and preserve the Faith."

"So," said Father, "like the Knights of old, you had a mission. And what became of this nameless bishop?"

"He's retired now, collecting his pension as we speak. I pray he makes his peace with God before he dies, and that's all that I can say about him. But I tell you this because I want you to understand how serious I am about the things that I do."

"You don't have to convince me," said Father. "Please continue."

"A few months ago," said Roundhead, "the enormity of the situation hit me. I couldn't let it go on, not without taking action, and I wanted to see that justice was done. So I sent word out on my network of influence: bring me Catholic relics and holy objects. My operatives are not thugs, Father. They are professional do-it men. They know that I will tolerate burglary, but not bodily injury. They are informed that I intend to reimburse every shopkeeper for his property damages, and they know I'm a stickler for precision—it would not please me to have to cover excessive property damage or medical expenses if anyone got injured. In this regard, the agent whose brash actions resulted in Mr. Slater's hospitalization will never work for me or any of my associates again. That was uncalled for. As for my more disciplined operatives, they also know that I will not brook thefts of relics from private individuals who have genuine devotion to them. But anyone possessing these treasures for frivolous, fraudulent, or sacrilegious purposes, whether knowingly or not, is fair game."

"Excuse me," said the gardener. "Why don't you just send your operatives to the shops and have them buy these things outright?"

"First," said Mr. Roundhead, "if the word got out—and it certainly would in this town—it would drive the prices sky-high. Such inflation could kindle the irreligious interest of art collectors and dealers, which would only compound the problem further and place these treasures beyond my reach. It's one thing to pay a shopkeeper's unreasonable price, but it's another to pay wholesale blackmail."

"I understand," said Father.

"Second," continued Roundhead, "there is the matter of justice. These shopkeepers deserve to be inconvenienced, if nothing else, because they dare to deal in the unbuyable. Even so, I see to it that their pains are short-lived. They all receive payment in full."

"Willie Kapps," said Father, "hasn't received any compensations for his inconveniences as far as I know."

"Willie Kapps," said Roundhead, "has nothing to do with what I'm talking about."

"You're positive about that," said Father.

"Quite. I know the man. I've done business with him personally on a number of occasions. But, knowing his field of 'expertise,' for want of a better term, I wouldn't think of causing him harm in any way. My life is cluttered enough without complicating it further with curses and spells."

"I understand," said Father. "So in due course, Catholic artifacts have been making their way to you through your network of operatives. I would imagine that by now you have quite a collection."

"I am not a collector," said Mr. Roundhead. "I consider myself a curator. This present generation doesn't want these things, but perhaps future generations will. The Roundheads will be watching, guarding, and protecting these treasures until that day arrives. Would you care to see the burden of which we find ourselves in charge?"

"I would," said Father. "Of course, if you show me these things, the rules of host and guest may become severely tested."

"I'm up for the challenge if you are. Mr. Feeney?"

"Where Father goes, I go," said the gardener, hoping he wouldn't regret those words.

"Then come with me," said Mr. Roundhead, rising from his chair. "I think you two, more than most, will appreciate what I have accomplished."

32

"GOOD LORD," GASPED THE GARDENER as we passed through another set of doors into what could only be described as a treasure chamber.

"Yes, He is," said Father, clasping his hands behind him, "or men would not have framed their devotion to Him in such profound fashion."

"Yes," beamed Mr. Roundhead, waving his arm around. "Yes, yes indeed."

It was like walking through a kaleidoscope of sparkling jewels and gleaming surfaces. There were chalices, ciboria, monstrances, patens, candlesticks, censers, tabernacles, reliquaries and much, much more. There were shelves and shelves cluttered with objects of gold and silver, studded with diamonds and glittering gems. There were also larger objects: baptismal fonts carved from single blocks of marble, entire altars of ornate stone or polished wood—the altar from Mr. Slater's warehouse was conspicuous among them, along with the lifelike statues we had admired two afternoons before. Everything was set in place with care, draped with fine silks, and craftily illuminated by hidden fluorescents.

Mr. Roundhead stood proudly beside a stone pedestal upon which rested something else I recognized from the brochure: nothing less than *Le San Pres'que Grall*—the 'next to the holy' cup once held by Saint Peter or Saint John. Considering the circs, did it really matter which? Surely any number of Christ's companions may have handled that ancient cup. Perhaps Saint Mary Magdalene helped set the table, or even Saint Martha, the woman who worried about so many things.

Eyes glistening, I strolled among the treasures, sniffing the scent of history, gawking at the mastery of so many artists who had put their talents to such fitting purposes.

To be honest, I was also looking for any sign of the lead coffin that I'd watched the Tumblars carry into the mausoleum Saturday morning. But after careful perusal, I could find no trace of the casket, nor any hint of the Relics of Saint Valeria.

"I repeat," said Mr. Roundhead as Father and I wandered back in his direction. "To the present generation, who have all but lost the Faith, these treasures are pearls cast before swine. This is not the first time the Church has experienced decline. We Roundheads helped rebuild Her before, and in due time, we will again."

"You'll forgive me for saying so," mumbled the gardener, perhaps a little louder than he'd anticipated—or perhaps not as loud as he would have preferred, "but it sounds a bit cockeyed to me."

"Be that as it may, Mr. Feeney," glared our host, "that's the way it is. Who do you think you are, anyway? You, too, Father. How dare you act so smug? What will you accomplish if you—Heaven forbid—have me arrested? If you manage to reveal the whereabouts of these things to the police, they will confiscate them. If the civil laws prevail, if you win your case in court, these treasures will be redistributed to the nonbelievers like so much vulgar merchandise, to end up as parlor decorations and bird feeders. Is that what you want to happen? Would you really expend your efforts to that end?"

"Go on," said Father. "I'm listening."

"But even so," continued Mr. Roundhead, "whereas you and your beloved judicial system would consign these holy objects to the garbage heap, I would not allow this to happen. If it came to a courtroom battle and I lost the first round, I would keep you tied up with so many appeals that you'd die of old age before you ever got a final judgment. By then no one would care any more, and in the mean time I'd find a way to legally claim them as my rightful property anyway. So I repeat: what can you hope to accomplish?"

"You may be right," said Father. "I think your methods are rash, dangerous, and unconscionable. But regarding the end to which you apply them—the preservation of precious relics—I'll have to give this a considerable amount of thought and prayer."

"You do that," said Mr. Roundhead. "And while you're considering the potential consequences of your actions, remember that even if you reveal the substance of this conversation to the police, and they proceed to come down on me, I assure you that they'll not find this place. You don't know where it is, and they never will. As to the present conversation, it would be your word as a controversial priest against mine as a prominent citizen and taxpayer."

"An unsettling prospect," agreed Father. "By the way, your assumptions regarding my attitude toward the judicial system are imprecise."

"I hoped so."

Mr. Roundhead motioned for us to return to his office.

"I don't want to be your enemy, Father," he said, resuming his place behind the desk. "These are desperate times, and in a strange way, we're on the same side. We're trying to preserve Tradition, you and I. As a priest, you're restricted by your office and your vows of obedience to your superiors. As a layman, I can do things you can never do. But you have impressed me, Father. You and your friend here showed some nerve coming to me this way, through the underground, not knowing who or what you would find. Which reminds me, Mr. Feeney. You've seen enough to reach your conclusions. Have you decided to sell me that relic of yours? You'll find me more than generous."

I looked at Father. He nodded his encouragement, but this did not convey what he was encouraging me to do. So, left to my own devices, I decided to be honest.

"No, Mr. Roundhead. I won't sell you this chip from the Crown of Thorns. I find you to be motivated by a uniquely Catholic Conscience—and I mean that in the positive sense of the word, not the topic of jokes that it has become in the popular mindset. Frankly, I find your methods offensive but your objectives honorable. Perhaps you are a Knight on a holy quest, to be judged by history as a hero rather than as a common criminal. These things are beyond me. But I will tell you this: I brought this relic only as a means of helping Father Baptist to gain access to you. Like I told Some Guy out there, it is the most precious material thing in my possession. I never intended to sell it, and I never will."

"Good," said Roundhead, opening an antique humidor and removing a fresh cigar. "I'd have been disappointed if you'd said otherwise."

"Something else is bothering me," I continued, ignoring his compliment. "People like Archibald Roring. You wouldn't know about him, but he's doubly victimized. Your 'agent' stole something from a pawnshop before he was able to raise the money to obtain it. Mr. Roring couldn't help it if his pastor sold the monstrance his dad donated to the parish—"

"In 1957," interrupted Mr. Roundhead, pointing to a report on his desk with the cigar while he dug around in his vest pocket for his clipper. "There's an inscription engraved on the base. Yes, I'm aware of Mr. Roring's situation, and I happen to remember Monsignor McManigill. He gave one of my cousins her First Holy Communion."

"You are thorough," I said. "I'll grant you that."

"I pay attention to details." Ceremoniously, he snipped the tip of his cigar into the Murkenmug and reached for an elegant gold-plated lighter. "Might you adjust your rancor if I told you that in due time my agents will contact Mr. Roring to discuss the return of the monstrance to him? I am not a common thief, Mr. Feeney, nor am I without compassion for the plight of the disfranchised laity. Every attempt will be made to restore such items to the families that donated them—if they still want them, and at no expense to them whatsoever."

"I suppose they'll have to sign a nondisclosure agreement," said Father.

Mr. Roundhead regarded Father as he drew the flame into his cigar and expelled several aromatic mushrooms of dense, gray smoke. "You're sharp, Father."

"I may be dull," said the gardener, his rancor apparently unadjusted, "but I still don't like it."

Our host tapped his ash into the hideous chalice.

I smiled in spite of myself.

"Well," said Father, "I guess that disposes of one item of business. Now I must bring up another, and for the sake of those rules of host and guest—not to mention the fate of a friend of ours—I need to ask you about your connection with the theft of the relics of Saint Valeria."

"I appreciate your candor, Father," said Mr. Roundhead. "I'll tell you this: after the way the cardinal ordered her body secreted away like that, I'd have leapt at the chance of securing her a fitting resting place. I'll admit that when you told me of the theft, I wondered if one of my operatives had developed initiative or gone overboard. I had the matter thoroughly checked out, and I can assure you that such was not the case. As it is, my agents have put out their feelers all over the city, but they've found no trace of Saint Valeria other than indications that she may have been shipped via airfreight to Rome. What information they procured with respect to your friend, Mr. Bontemps, they have reported to the police. Your trail to save him does not pass by here."

"That," admitted Father, "is disappointing."

"So," said Mr. Roundhead, "we know better where we stand, you and I. There doesn't seem to be much more we can do for each other at the moment, so I suggest we bring this meeting to a close."

"Well," said Father, reaching inside his cassock and pulling out a bulging envelope. "There is one other item of business. Martin and I did not come here with entirely empty hands."

"What's this?" asked Mr. Roundhead, hefting the envelope and carefully scrutinizing the wax congealed along the flap. "This appears to be Fulbright's seal."

"You've done business with him before," observed Father. "You recognize his mark."

"And his style. Should I open it?"

"Your choice," said Father. "It's the cardinal's cash offer for the return of the Murkenstein Chalice."

"Really," said Roundhead, smiling as though savoring a prize lobster. He broke the seal, peeked inside, then whistled. "All this—just for the one cup? No mention of the four reliquaries? No concern for *Le San Pres'que Grall?*"

"None," said Father. "His interest in the matter is decisively focused."

"The old boy must really be squirming."

"As pleasant as that thought may be to you," said Father, "and as tempting as it may be to prolong the moment, I suggest you consider that if Cardinal Fulbright gets what he wants immediately, he's not likely to pursue the matter further. On the other hand, the longer he waits, the more consumed he will become with his desire—not just for his chalice, but for revenge."

"You have a point there, Father," said Mr. Roundhead, reaching down behind his desk. He came up with what appeared to be an athletic bag, the kind used by tennis players. Grabbing the Murkenmug, he over-ended it above the wastebasket. He tapped it a few times to dislodge some of the ashes, realized that they were more stubborn than he had thought, then unceremoniously stuffed the cup inside the nylon bag, which he then handed across the desk to Father. "I'd say we have a deal."

"Very well," said Father. "I will hand this over to the cardinal in short order."

"And that," said Mr. Roundhead, "concludes our business. I trust that you will consider carefully all that we have discussed."

"Of course," said Father, getting up from his chair. "I guess we'll be going, Martin."

"You can find your way back to the limousine," said Mr. Roundhead with no pretense of a final handshake. "Through those doors and down the corridor. Mr. Guy will see to your safe return."

I must admit that I felt a curious reluctance at leaving the underground fortress—all those treasures, all those moral dilemmas. It was the stuff of life: beauty, devotion, and the clash of principles. And, to be frank, it had felt good to bask in the shimmer of so many Catholic artifacts. Sort of like visiting the Vatican Museum only you don't have to stay behind the ropes.

"Well, Martin?" said Father as Mr. Guy whooshed us off in our shaded, curtained cocoon.

"This certainly has been an exciting evening, Father. But even with all the adrenaline and rigmarole, we have been of no use to Pierre."

"I must admit," sighed Father, eyes glistening in the dark, "my hunch did not pay off. But we're not licked yet. I'll just have to go at his problem from another angle."

"In a strange way, though," I mused, grabbing the seat as the limo made a sharp right turn at high speed, "I think that, with a little taming, Roderick Roundhead could almost be Tumblar material."

"Indeed," laughed Father. "I was thinking the same thing myself."

Tuesday, November Fourteenth

Feast Day of Saint Laurence O'Toole
Abbot of Glendalough, later Archbishop of Dublin.
Seven dead persons were raised to life
at his tomb (1180 AD)

33

IT WAS FIFTY-SEVEN MINUTES PAST MIDNIGHT when Some Guy gunned the accelerator of the longest of limos and tore away down the back alley behind Saint Philomena's, leaving us standing in the tiny back parking lot. The first thing we noticed was our very own Jeep in its usual slot—returned, apparently, by one of Mr. Roundhead's agents. Anxiously, I found my keys in my pocket which Mr. Guy had graciously returned, yanked the door open, and checked around inside to see if anything was missing. That's when I noticed the time. It's indelibly etched in my mind in large, rectangular, luminous green digits: 12:57.

The reason I'm making a point of this is that there had never been a digital clock in the dashboard before. For that matter, the stereo cassette/compact disc player was new, too.

"And new tires," I said, emerging from the car and looking it over.

"Michelins," said Father. "Not bad."

"Even the rear-mounted spare!" I scratched my head. "What is this—some kind of macabre reverse vandalism?"

"I don't know," said Father. "I wonder when they returned our Jeep, and why the upgrade. Perhaps Monsignor Havermeyer knows something, but the lights are out in his RV. Maybe he's asleep, or perhaps we'll find him in the rectory.

And that's exactly where we did find him, sitting in my favorite chair's twin in Father's study, pondering a huge, old, tattered volume on moral theology. Janos Prachenski, S.J.'s omnibus, no less. Heavy stuff.

"Well, Monsignor," said Father. "Burning the midnight oil, I see."

"Something is puzzling me," said Havermeyer. "But I can't find anything close to an answer in here."

"Something to do with Archibald Roring?" I asked, noticing that the monsignor also had a copy of *The Vampire: His Kith and Kin* by Montague Summers on his lap, under the larger book.

"Martin," he said, closing the Prachenski. As he did so, the edge of *The Dark Night of the Soul* by Saint John of the Cross also came into view. And he said something was merely puzzling him?

"Yes, Mon Señor," I answered.

"You know I cannot discuss anything said under the seal of the confessional."

"I wouldn't think of asking you to," I said, embarrassed that I had unintentionally crossed a line, yet not so sure that I had.

"I wouldn't either," said Father Baptist, easing himself into his chair behind the desk, "but I would like to know, Monsignor—for pastoral reasons—whether Mr. Roring's spiritual needs were ... addressed."

"This much I'll say," said Havermeyer who, after all, was from the old school. Even in his Modernist days, he was a stickler for the confidentiality of the Sacrament of Confession. In his opinion, a priest should not even admit the *identity* of the penitent, let alone ever reveal his secrets.

"Yes, Monsignor?" said Father, lifting his pipe and pouch out of the top drawer.

"I dropped by the hospital earlier this evening," said Havermeyer. "I looked in on your friend, Willie Kapps. He's still unconscious, though the nurses told me that they've observed his fingers and toes twitching from time to time. They said that's a good sign. Then I visited a patient on a lower floor. We spoke for quite a while. It was most ... well ... I can't go into it."

"I know what you mean," said Father. "That's one of the thorns of the priestly vocation. Sometimes silence can be exhausting."

"And irritating," said the gardener, flopping himself down in his favorite chair. The springs squawked in protest.

"I was hoping to find an answer to something in these books," said Havermeyer, getting up and inserting Saint John of the Cross into a vacant slot on the bookshelf, "but it eludes me."

"There again," said Father, pushing a pinch of tobacco into the bowl of his pipe with his thumb, "I know what you mean. I went in search of a solution tonight. What I found was an answer that reveals much but helps with nothing. The key that I seek eludes me."

Monsignor pushed the volume on moral theology into a rectangular vacancy on a lower shelf.

"Well," said Father, as if reaching a decision, "there's one thing I need to do. No use putting it off." He picked up the telephone and dialed—yes, we still have a rotary phone—*dialed* a number. As he listened for an answer, he struck a match and took several long draws on his pipe. He tossed the match into the ashtray.

"Ah, hello," he said presently. "Morgan, this is Father John Baptist. I apologize for the lateness of the hour ... oh, quite right ... for the *earliness* of the hour. I must speak with Mr. Roundhead on a matter of importance. Oh? Do put him on, please."

Father cupped the receiver and winked at me. "He says Mr. Roundhead is expecting my call."

"Probably bluffing," I whispered. "I bet he tells that to everyone who calls at this time of night—just to throw them off guard."

"Father Baptist, Mr. Roundhead," he said, returning his attention to the phone. "I'm calling to tell you that I've decided that I won't tell the police about what you have stored under your home near the Hollywood Reservoir ...That's what I said. You know the place. Mr. Feeney and I paid a visit to you there yesterday afternoon, and again a short while ago. No, I won't tell you how I know. No, and that's final. I'm calling, as I said, to assure you that I won't tell the authorities—for the present. I suggest that, in anticipation of the event that I should have a change of heart, you take precautions. I think we understand each other, Mr. Roundhead ... Excuse me. What's that you said? ... Oh really."

Father covered the mouthpiece and said to me, "Progress report from his field agents. The crate from LAX arrived in Rome yesterday afternoon. By the time Mr. Roundhead's agents got there, it had already been claimed."

Suddenly his attention snapped back to the phone. He set down his pipe and snatched up a pencil. "What name did you say? Spell that please. Got it. Okay, Mr. Roundhead.

Thank-you for the information. Good night—no, good morning to you, sir. And Mary keep you."

He set the receiver down in the cradle.

He looked at me.

I looked at him.

Monsignor Havermeyer was standing thoughtfully by the bookcase, the vampire book by Montague Summers open again in his hands. He turned a page, scrunched his eyebrows, and released a long, weary sigh.

"So," I said at last to Father, "how did you know where his vault was?"

"Easy." He picked up his pipe and struck another match. "The gate guard we met on the way in, you will recall, had a particularly noisy set of keys. I heard them again this evening, clear as a bell, when the limo passed by his guardhouse as we approached our destination."

"The guard must have an awfully long shift," I observed, "to be at his post from morning to midnight."

"Or he hands his keys to his replacement. In any case, I was right or Mr. Roundhead wouldn't have reacted the way he did just now."

"Meanwhile," I mused, "he's probably wringing Some Guy's neck for letting you sneak in a homing device concealed in your belly button."

"Perhaps," smiled Father, drawing the match's flame into the bowl of his pipe. The tobacco hissed and smoldered with a somber red glow.

"And who did he say picked up the crate at the airport?"

"Ah," said Father, exhaling a flower of blossoming smoke, "a very good point you raise, Martin. A very good point. Excuse me." He picked up the phone and dialed again. "Father Nicanor. Sorry to trouble you at this hour ... Well thank-you, I appreciate that."

GARDENING TIPS: Father Stephen Nicanor: age unknown (perhaps indeterminable in years as we know them), pastor at Saint Basil's Maronite Catholic Church, mystic, Father Baptist's friend and confessor. Father Nicanor speaks eleven languages, holds five doctorates, and is said to have celebrated Mass on seven continents. Yes, all seven.

                                              --M.F.

F.Y.I.: The Maronites are an ancient but
inconspicuous Rite within the Roman Catholic Church--perfectly valid, loyal to the
Holy Father, and for the most part unrav-
aged by the changes that have plagued the
Roman Rite--Father Baptist's and mine--
since Vatican II.

"Listen," Father was saying, "don't the Maronites have a
major house in Rome? ... Yes ... Would you say that you,
yourself, are well-connected over there? ... Well, tell me this:
does the name Raphael Zaiden mean anything to you? ... Oh,
really ... That is most enlightening ... I'd like to go into it but
time is pressing. No, I'll be discrete—count on it. Yes.
Thanks again, Father. Goodnight."

"Zaiden?" I said as Father cradled the phone. "Isn't that
the doctor Arthur was talking about? The one with the clinic
in Italy?"

"Well," said Father, leaning back in his chair, "Arthur
definitely did mention his name, but he's not a doctor spe-
cializing in the treatment of narcolepsy."

"No? Then what is he?"

"Father Nicanor's uncle, for one thing."

"His uncle? And how would Father Nicanor's uncle be
connected with all this, and if he's not a doctor, what is he?
And why would Pierre send a crate to him? And if all that's
so, then why did Arthur lie to us about who he's taking his
sister to see?"

"It is getting thick, I'll admit," said Father. "Let's concentrate on Pierre for a moment. Frankly, I don't know what
to do, Martin. I had a strong hunch that Roderick Roundhead
was the key to the whole puzzle. I was fairly sure that he
would be the man at the end of our quest for Saint Valeria,
and therefore the answer to Pierre's predicament. Mr.
Roundhead is wealthy enough to have influence above and
below ground. He is interested enough—indeed, desperate
enough—to save the legacy of his family. He'd already purchased a number of treasures from Cardinal Fulbright outright. And, most telling of all, he was also noble enough to
risk discovery. In spite of fears that we might be onto him, he
let us approach, I think, because of your brilliant stipulation
that you be allowed to change your mind if you deemed the
buyer dishonorable!"

"Well," I said, "I don't know how *brilliant* it was. I thought the prize for the brightest light bulb went to you when you said that the man who would desire to possess the 'next to the Grail' *and* who would fall for my 'brilliant stipulation' would be the sort of man who would go to great lengths to get his hands on the relics of Saint Valeria."

"And though I've no doubt that he would if he could," said Father, "I believe him when he says he hasn't. Where could she be, Martin? What's Arthur up to? What in Heaven's name is Pierre hiding? What am I missing?"

34

MONSIGNOR HAVERMEYER, having given up on vampires, shoved Montague Summers into his slot on the shelf. Then, as he turned back to his chair, he noticed the three volumes Edward had dropped by the other night still sitting on Father Baptist's desk.

"Excuse me, Father," he said, tapping the books with his fingertips, "do you want me to put these away while I'm at it?"

"Let me see," said Father, taking up the top volume and cracking it open. "Ah, yes. *The Incorruptibles* by Joan Carroll Cruz. I love this book. It never ceases to amaze me how some Saints' bodies never underwent decomposition in the grave."

"I've heard about such things," said Monsignor Havermeyer. "I always thought they were just pious fables. But, good Heavens, look!" He leaned forward to examine the photograph on the open page in Father's hands. "I've never read this book. Perhaps I should. You mean, they never—you know—after they died?"

"It varies," said Father, thumbing through the pages. "You see? Some undergo minor changes, some look almost like mummies, and then you get the occasional one who, centuries after their death, remain as supple to the touch as the day they died. Just the sight of them has been known to produce conversions."

"I don't think it's in that particular book," said the gardener, "but my favorite is still the tongue of Saint Anthony of Padua. The rest of him crumbled away, but when they opened his tomb, there was his tongue—pink and pliable as the day he died. He must've been quite a talker. They even gave his tongue a feast day."

"You're kidding," said Havermeyer.

"February 15th," smiled Father Baptist, closing the book and handing it to Monsignor Havermeyer. "Check your Latin missal, Monsignor, if you don't believe me. And let's see—what else was our studious Tumblar reading? *Martyrs of the Catholic Faith.* Hm, I wonder if Saint Valeria is in here ... Well, she is, but it's just a brief article, nothing comprehensive. Hold on, there's a footnote here, referencing the 1913 *Catholic Encyclopedia.*"

"That must be a rare edition," said Monsignor Havermeyer.

"It is," said Father, "but it's the only one I have. See? What do you know?" He set down *Martyrs* and took up the third and last volume in the stack of returned books. I could see the gold letters on the black leather spine: VOLUME XV: TOUR-ZW. Father shuffled through the delicate onionskin pages, then spread the book open on his desk.

"Here she is," said Father, pointing to an article on the right side. "Saint Valeria, Virgin and Martyr."

"And that's her picture?" asked Havermeyer, leaning close.

"Apparently," said Father, moving his hand to reveal a black-and-white photograph on the opposite page. He squinted at the fine print. "'Saint Valeria seen in repose,'" he read, taking up his pipe while he read aloud, "'at her cathedral in Rome in 1874, shortly before her ... removal ... to ... Los Angeles ...'" His voice trailed off, as though the words were triggering other thoughts in his head. He drew a circle around the photograph with his finger.

"Hm," said Havermeyer, "she almost looks like ... what year does it say she died in?"

"363," said Father absently. Then he blinked and said it again, purposefully. "363. I wonder, could it be ...?"

Suddenly Father Baptist put his pipe down and snatched up the phone again. "Hello, Sergeant Wickes? Father Baptist. I had a feeling you might be working late tonight ... Hm? I appreciate your saying so. No, I understand that you're just doing your job ... Look, you've been reconstructing the movements of the Tumblars Saturday evening, haven't you? Well, have you checked to see when Arthur's sister's flight arrived at LAX? Was it at five, as Arthur told us? ... Is that so? Okay, Sergeant. Thank-you."

"Something amiss?" I asked.

Father pulled open a drawer, consulted a sheet of expensive-looking parchment, then dialed another number. "I have to confirm something. It looks like this is my night for shaking people out of bed."

"Who are you calling?" I asked.

"Mrs. von Derschmidt?" he said into the receiver. "I'm terribly sorry to disturb you at this hour. This is Father John Baptist ... Yes, 'Arthur's priest friend' in Los Angeles ... Oh he has? That's very gratifying ... And how's the weather in Cleveland? That bad ... Well, the reason I'm calling is that I need a bit of information, and Arthur is indisposed at the moment. I just want to know which flight your daughter, Beth, took when she came to Los Angeles three days ago. Yes, that would be helpful." He scribbled a three-digit number with his pencil. "Very good. No, Mrs. von Derschmidt, that's all I need. No, nothing's wrong. No doubt Arthur will call to explain a little later. Okay, thank-you and good morning."

"How is it that you happen to have Arthur's mother's telephone number?" I asked as he set down the phone.

"The Tumblars gave me this list some time ago," he said, indicating the sheet of parchment before closing the drawer. "Insurance numbers, family members to contact, that sort of thing. Don't forget that these gentlemen go all over town involving themselves in social affairs so that at any propitious moment they can turn the topic of conversation to the Catholic Faith. That is their mission, their apostolate."

"I know," I said. "I've seen them in action."

"Given the circs," said Father, "one can imagine the situation arising where things could get, shall we say, intense. They gave me this information just in case any of them wound up injured, hospitalized or worse."

"Oh," I said. "Not a bad precaution."

Father reached down behind his desk, brought up a telephone directory, and plopped it down in front of him. He peeled it open and ran his finger down a page. Finding what he wanted, he snatched up the phone again.

"What's he up to?" asked Monsignor Havermeyer, slipping *Martyrs of the Catholic Faith* into its niche on the shelf.

"You've got me," sighed the gardener.

"TWA?" said Father into the phone. "I just have a question. Could you please tell me when flight 584 from Cleveland landed at LAX on Saturday last? Yes, I'll wait." He drummed his fingers impatiently. "2:37 you say? Thank-you, you've been most helpful."

"Well?" asked myself and the monsignor in unison.

"There was a flight, number 867, from Cleveland to Los Angeles that arrived at 5:05 on Saturday," said Father, rubbing his hands together. "But Mrs. von Derschmidt says that she saw her daughter off at the airport herself, and she remembers the flight number as 584. Flight 584, according to the reservation clerk at TWA, landed at LAX at 2:37 in the afternoon."

"When the Tumblars came by here at dinner time to introduce us to Beth," I said, "they said they were just then on their way home from the airport. I think Arthur mentioned earlier that day that her flight was due at 5 o'clock. But you say Beth's plane landed at 2:37. Why would Arthur and the others lie about it?"

"Good question," said Father, "and it begs another. I need to get information on the passenger list for a future flight. The airlines consider that sort of thing confidential. I know that Mr. Roundhead's operatives have had success penetrating the airline computers, but I don't want to call him back—not for this. Think, Martin. Who do we know who's got chops at the computer?"

He looked at me.

I looked at him.

"Sybil Wexler," we said together.

"I hate to do this," he said, snatching up the phone again. Glancing at her card on his desk, he cranked the dial. "It'll put her in a peculiar situation, but ... Hello, Sybil. Father Baptist. I thought you might be putting in some overtime. Can you speak freely? Excellent. Look, I understand about your situation with Tragg, and I also know that you're an honest woman."

He started scribbling little circles with his pencil. As he spoke the circles got darker and darker as he pressed harder and harder. "The problem is that I need you to find out something for me, and once you have the information, I'm asking you not to act upon it for twenty-four hours. Can I have your assurance on that? No, I can't tell you what I'm after until I have your word. Do I have it? Yes, I understand ... Good. You're at your computer terminal now? Okay, I need you to access flight reservations for the next, say, three days. I don't know which airline, so you'll have to scan them all. I realize it will take a few minutes to get in. I'll hold on until you're ready."

"What's he up to?" asked Monsignor Havermeyer again, easing himself back into his chair, his librarian duties completed.

"Beats me," I shrugged. "When he gets this way—"

"Martin," said Father.

"Yes, Father."

"Where's that phone Ernie gave me?"

"You should know," I said, indicating the mysterious folds of his cassock. "Somewhere in there, I suppose. Some Guy returned it before he drove off."

"Ah," he said, hunching his right shoulder to hold the phone to his ear while he fished around inside his cassock. Discovering the device, he pulled it out and fumbled with the buttons. Then he held it up to his left ear. "Mrs. Wong? Father John Baptist. I'm terribly sorry to wake you at this hour. I must speak with your husband. Yes, I'll wait."

"He's calling Solomon Yung-sul Wong," I explained to Monsignor Havermeyer, "the county coroner."

"Look at me," said Father, his face framed with the two phones. This peculiar arrangement—right shoulder hunched to hold one phone, opposite hand raised to hold the other—left his right hand free to scribble his maniacal doodles. "I could get used to this."

"He's joking, of course," said the gardener.

"Yes, Sybil," said Father, turning his attention to his right ear. "Okay, I want you to see if the people I'm about to name have booked any outbound flights. I'll also want their destinations—" Something snapped in his hand. "Darn, just a second. I've broken my pencil."

Glaring at the point that had dared to buckle, Father tossed the implement into the wastebasket. He pulled open his drawer, rummaged around furiously, then slammed it shut again.

"Martin," he huffed, "run to the kitchen—will you?—and get me a pencil. Millie keeps a supply in the drawer next to the fridge."

"Sure," I said, groping my way to my wobbly legs, reluctant to miss anything. I lumbered and lurched my way to the kitchen and, sure enough, there was a half-empty package of sharpened number twos right where Father said there'd be. Taking several as insurance against more dark circles, I headed back to the study.

As I returned I saw the phone receiver sitting idle in its cradle next to Father's pipe. Blast! I'd missed his interchange with Sybil Wexler. I also noticed a fountain pen in his right hand, and a bunch of illegible squiggles on his note pad made by same. Monsignor Havermeyer had, no doubt, come to the rescue in my absence.

"That you, Solomon?" Father was saying into the cell phone. "Yes, I'm aware of the time, and I apologize. I need to know something. Did you perform the autopsy on Roger Galloway? That's right, the guard at the mausoleum. What did you find? I know the rules, Solomon, but it's *me* for Heaven's sake. Tell me! ... Is that right? You're absolutely certain? There can be no doubt? You'd better spell that for me."

Ignoring my pencils, Father wrote down three long words with Monsignor Havermeyer's fountain pen. Unlike the hieroglyphics on the rest of the page, Father printed each letter distinctly and carefully. I twisted my head to see them: SPONTANEOUS SUBARACHNOID HEMORRHAGE.

It was still ancient Egyptian as far as I was concerned.

"Got it," said Father into the receiver. "Solomon, I can't express my thanks enough ... Yes, I'll start by letting you and your wife go back to sleep. Good-bye."

"So what did the coroner find?" asked Havermeyer as Father clicked off the cell phone and set it down with finality.

"Exactly what I was beginning to suspect," said Father. "Now I'm sure. Monsignor, Martin, I've just solved the case."

"You have?" squeaked the gardener. "Great. Let's celebrate."

"Well," said Father, "there are a few formalities we must see to first."

"Such as?" asked Havermeyer.

"Like," said Father, "getting Pierre out of jail, and locating one missing Saint."

"Oh, that," said the gardener, settling back in his favorite chair. "Wake me when you've disposed of those minor details, will you, Father?"

"Don't get comfortable, Martin," said Father, handing the fountain pen to the monsignor. "You and I are going places."

"And what about me?" asked Havermeyer, pocketing his pen.

"I have an errand for you, Monsignor," said Father, reaching for the pen that was no longer on his desk. Frowning, he grabbed one of the pencils I had retrieved from the kitchen. Opening the desk drawer, he consulted the parchment the Tumblars had thoughtfully provided. Then he scribbled something on a fresh sheet of paper, tore it off, and handed it to Havermeyer. "I want you to go to this first address. You will find someone there. Make whatever overtures you must—say there's been a terrible accident, whatever—but bring that person to this second location, and be sure you arrive at exactly this time. The timing is critical, so I'm depending on you."

"Me?" inquired Monsignor Havermeyer, inflated with responsibility, examining the squiggles on the page. He frowned, then sniffed, then folded the paper into his pocket. "I'll do my best, Father. But I must confess I don't see what you learned from all those phone calls that adds up to a solution."

"They don't," said Father, "but they support my hypothesis."

"Which is?" asked the gardener, preparing to rise painfully to his feet again.

"And to think," mused Father, ignoring my question, "that the key to the whole thing has been sitting here on my desk since Sunday evening. Edward provided the answer when he returned those books. It's so obvious, I wonder if he intended it that way."

Suddenly, Father shook himself into action. He reached down behind the desk and hefted the nylon bag containing the fabulous—or rather fatuous—Murkenmug. "Let's go."

"What key?" I asked, gripping my cane for support. "What answer?"

"Martin," said Father, grabbing my arm and herding me toward the door. "I'll show you. And let me tell you something: this is going to blow your mind, for want of a better term."

"Oh goodie," I said doubtfully as he pulled me down the hallway.

35

"YOU'RE SURE YOU WON'T TELL ME what happened?" inquired Father Baptist, leaning forward in the rickety chair.

"I'm not going to talk about it," said Pierre, seated across from him. "At least, not yet."

We were back in the interrogation room at police headquarters. There were just Father, Pierre, and myself. The rest of the Tumblars, we were informed, had hung around the station until after midnight. They had finally gone home an hour before.

"Then when?" demanded Father.

"When it's time, you'll know," said Pierre, rubbing his sleepless eyes with his palms. He lowered his hands and looked Father Baptist square in the face. "You will understand, Father. You will not agree, but you will understand."

"You say that as if you're sure of me," said Father sternly.

"I am, Father."

"And if I don't agree when I find out what you've been up to, what am I to do?"

"I know you'll stand by me," said Pierre, his voice steady as a stone.

"Even if I don't agree?" asked Father.

"I know you'll stand by me precisely because, whether you agree or disagree, you will most assuredly understand."

"I'm beginning to think I will," said Father, lowering his head and rubbing the back of his neck. Suddenly he looked up. "Very well, Pierre, if you had played this my way, we'd both have fun. But since you've insisted on playing it your way, I'll have fun. I ought to wallop you for putting us through all this."

"I don't understand," said Pierre.

"And you probably won't agree," said Father, "but here's what's going to happen. My attorney, Mr. Drew de Montfort, has sworn out a writ of *habeas corpus*. The police either have to charge you with something or turn you loose. I've already had a long talk with Lieutenant Taper and Sergeant Wickes. Since they're not prepared to bring formal charges against you at this time, you're free to go. And you're coming with me."

"What if I don't want to?" asked Pierre.

"Like I said," said Father, standing, "at your insistence, I'll now have fun. Surely, knowing me as you do, you'll not want me blustering around in Tumblar affairs without you along as chaperone, eh?"

"You've got a point there, Father," said Pierre, climbing to his full height. "Perhaps I should go with you."

"Good," said Father. "You're finally beginning to show a modicum of sense."

As we stepped outside into the corridor, Lieutenant Taper, who had propped himself against the wall, propelled himself to an erect position with a shove of his left leg. "That didn't take long."

"No," agreed Father. "I pulled rank."

"Whatever works," said Taper, smiling wearily. He dug into his pocket and produced something small and rectangular. I tried to see what it was as he handed it to Father Baptist, but all I glimpsed was a blur as it disappeared into the mysterious folds of Father's cassock.

"Thanks, Larry," said Father. "I'll return this within a few hours."

"And as for you," said Larry Taper to Pierre Bontemps, " I sincerely hope that you won't be back."

"From your lips to God's ears, Lieutenant," said Pierre.

"We have to hurry," said Father. "We have a schedule to keep."

36

"WHY HAVE WE COME HERE?" asked Pierre, eyes wide and anxious as I pulled the Jeep into a slot in the central parking lot at Los Angeles International Airport.

"To see off a friend," said Father.

"I don't understand," said Pierre, not very convincingly.

"And you won't agree," said the gardener as we made our way toward the sign that said INTERNATIONAL DEPARTURES. "But we've been all over that."

It didn't take long to go through the security gate, not at that time of morning. One guard, who reminded me of a dog I once ran off with my cane, took pronounced interest in the reliquary in my pocket when it made the metal detectors bleep. I'd forgotten that I still had it on me and was shocked that, contrary to previous experience, it was now detectable by their instruments. Only when I produced my authentication papers did he let me pass, and then only after getting an okay from his superior, who reminded me of a cat that once scratched me.

Pierre, I noted, had to hand his glassless monocle to the guard before he could pass through.

Father Baptist stepped through the gate beepless, like a thief in the night—his cassock mysteriously cloaking the Rosaries and other metal objects I knew had to be concealed in there somewhere. Whatever his charm, he must have left it turned off when Some Guy was putting us through the wringer.

"I wonder why my reliquary set off the alarm this time," I whispered to Father. "It didn't the last time I carried it through security. And now you go waltzing through with enough metal on you to build a car."

"For myself, I've no idea," said he. "As for your splinter from the Crown of Thorns, during your last airport experience it was housed in a tiny case wrapped in that regal cloth the bishop gave you. This time it's in a golden vessel the size of my fist."

"Well, there is that. But it doesn't explain you."

"One of life's mysteries," he smiled.

"What gate are we looking for?"

"As always," mused Father, "the one at the farthest end of the terminal."

"I should have known."

For several minutes we walked in silence, Father taking purposeful strides, Pierre taking dubious ones, and yours truly struggling behind.

At last we came to the large, circular waiting area at the end of the terminal. People of all sorts and descriptions were scattered among rows of molded plastic chairs, baggage clustered around their feet, candy wrappers clutched in their hands, children moaning that they had to go to the bathroom for the thousandth time.

"*TWA flight 1326 bound for Rome, Italy, will begin boarding in approximately twenty minutes,*" said the voice of a woman who sounded as though she was gripping her nose. "*We will be boarding the plane in sections, so please have your boarding passes ready.*"

A few people scrambled for their tickets, but the vast majority, realizing that there was still plenty of time, simply settled back into their communal coma.

"I don't see them," said the gardener.

"I do," said Father. "There, over at the far window."

And indeed there they were, off by themselves, detached from the rest of the crowd. Joel Maruppa, Jonathan Clubb, Edward Strypes Wyndham and Arthur von Derschmidt were grouped around a wheelchair, their backs toward us, their attention riveted on a jumbo jet that was just roaring down the runway. They were all dressed in casual clothes, which was why I didn't spot them at first, unused as I was to seeing them in anything but formalwear.

"Father, please," whispered Pierre, gripping Father's arm. "Don't interfere."

"It is because I've interfered," countered Father, "that you're here and not still at police headquarters."

"But that was unimportant," hissed Pierre.

"I understand," said Father, "but I don't agree. You should be here with your friends. Lord knows you've risked enough for the privilege."

"Just what are you going to do?"

Father increased his pace. "I'm going to march right up to those fellows like this, and then I'm going to—"

"You'll spoil it," said Pierre, hurrying up beside him. "You'll ruin everything."

"We'll see," said Father, walking even faster.

Like a relative who had arrived in the nick of time to say good-bye, Father Baptist bounded up to the huddled Tumblars, slapped several on the back, laughed in their startled faces, and clasped Arthur von Derschmidt's hand.

"Arthur, Arthur!" exclaimed Father Baptist, all jovial and *bon voyage*-ish. "We almost didn't make it in time! It would have been such a shame if you had taken off—against police admonitions to remain in the city, by the way—before we got a chance to say good-bye."

"Father Baptist," said Arthur, his breath preceding his tongue so it sounded more like a choke.

"Oh, no," moaned Joel.

"How did you find us?" winced Edward. "How did you know—?"

"We were so careful," sputtered Jonathan.

"And," said Father, turning his attention to the beautiful woman asleep in the wheelchair, her long black hair falling gently around her shoulders. "How is your sister, Valeria?"

They all gasped in unison. The sudden lack of oxygen in the immediate area made the gardener momentarily dizzy, but he recovered quickly—until the reality of what had just been said hit him. Then the real vertigo commenced.

What had Father said as we were leaving the rectory? *This is going to blow your mind, for want of a better term.* Well, it couldn't have been better phrased. Saint Valeria, Patroness of Los Angeles, was sitting there in a wheelchair—in the flesh, though not in spirit. Until that moment, I'd never had any picture in my mind of her other than a simple lead-lined coffin, or passing thoughts of the bones and dust I'd assumed it contained. It hadn't occurred to me that Saint Valeria might be the occasional one *who, centuries after their death, remain as supple to the touch as the day they died.*

Yes, as I looked at the sleeping woman under those bright lights, I could see that she was perhaps a little more than asleep. Indeed, she had not breathed in many centuries. Still, she looked as soft and gentle and holy as the day she was martyred in the year 363 when Julian the Apostate failed to convince her to give up either her Faith or her chastity.

No wonder the people protested her removal from her cathedral in Rome. No wonder Father had said that this was going to blow my mind. From that moment on in this story, consider it blown, for want of a better term. But even such moments of elevated awareness pass, and within five beats of my heart I was back on the ground, considering the metaphysical limitations of coarse matter.

"Wait a minute," I found myself saying. "If this is indeed Saint Valeria, and this is who we've been seeing in the company of the Tumblars, then who was the girl we met at Arthur's last night?"

"Hold on," said Father. "Let's not get ahead of ourselves. Pierre has said emphatically that I wouldn't agree but that I would understand. I propose to put his assertion to a test, and to do that I've got to first clear away the fog that surrounds this mystery."

"Go ahead, Father," said Pierre, sinking into a molded plastic chair. "It's your show."

"Not mine," said Father. "Yours. And quite a tale it is."

37

THEIR OPTIONS SOMEWHAT RESTRICTED at this juncture, the Tumblars gathered around to hear Father's narrative. Arthur and Edward rested their hands on the woman's shoulders as they listened, as if providing a departing relative a dose of moral support. We no doubt looked, from the perspective of all the travelers who were awaiting their flight, very homey and familial over by the window.

"I'll begin with a ghost story," said Father, lowering his voice as though we were huddled around a campfire. "Or rather, a tale of the undead. There was once a man by the name of Archibald Roring, an investment counselor by trade and a Catholic by Grace. It had come to his attention that the pastor of his church had sold a number of priceless vessels and relics to a pawnbroker named Goodman. Indignant and enraged, Roring was in the process of pooling sufficient funds to purchase said objects from Mr. Goodman, but his plan collapsed when I informed him that the pawnshop had been burglarized and the sacred treasures stolen. This, coupled with a newspaper article about the removal of Saint Valeria from the cathedral to the mausoleum at New Golgotha Cemetery, and compounded by a thrashing interrogation by Lieutenant Tragg Holcomb and Officer Sybil Wexler, left Mr. Roring in a tumultuous emotional state. His turmoil was further enflamed by a generous application of alcohol at Darby's."

The Tumblars shifted their weight from foot to foot, unsure where this was leading.

"Thus fueled by drink, and compelled by desperation," continued Father, "Archibald Roring drove to the cemetery. Inebriated as he was, I doubt that he had any specific plan in mind. Driven by emotions, in other words, he parked his car just outside the front gates, which he found chained but not locked. Letting himself in, he made his way toward the mausoleum, groping his way between the large stone monuments in that section of the park. It was there, amidst the clutter of tombstones and in the gloom of descending night, that he saw something that almost cost him his sanity."

"What could he have seen?" asked Jonathan. "We were only—"

"What he saw," said Father, "was a procession of spectral beings in black tailcoats carrying a coffin out of the mausoleum. Imagine the man's horror when he observed these vampire-like forms prying the casket open, then proceeding to lift out the body of a beautiful girl. He watched in utter terror as they carefully arranged her in the back seat of a waiting station wagon. From his vantage point, for all he knew, she had just been brought to life, raised from death by a group of vampires. Perhaps it did not register on his feverish mind that she was limp and lifeless. Perhaps the movements of the gathered vampires obscured his vision, allowing his mind to fill in grisly details that weren't there. In any case, the poor man either swooned or knocked himself out on a headstone, to be revived later when the police arrived."

"This is unbelievable," said Jonathan.

"Tell that to Mr. Roring," said Father. "It's going to take a lot of counseling—mine, not some psychiatrist's—to convince him otherwise."

"We had no idea he was there," said Edward.

"Nonetheless, he was," said Father. "We will leave him to his disturbed nightmares, for these tailcoated grave robbers then built a crate for the coffin right there on the asphalt drive. The coffin secure in its wooden shipping crate, they hefted it into the back of Edward's van. While they busied themselves with a hurried clean-up—not a thorough job, mind you, since the police later found splinters and nails at the scene—Pierre went into the mausoleum to cement the facing stone back in place in the crypt. Some time during those labors, and unbeknownst to him, the plain glass lens got dislodged from Pierre's monocle, to be crushed by his own foot in the dark. Then, setting his gold ring on the top edge of the facing stone as before, and gathering up his tools, Pierre made his exit."

"Excuse me," said the gardener, shifting his cane from one hand to the other, "all of that prying and hammering would have made a considerable racket. Surely the guards would have heard the noise and investigated."

"The guards," said Father, "were in on the whole thing—Roberto and Duggo, anyway. Of them I'm sure, and they'll have some explaining to do, at least to me. They persuaded the regular guards to take the night off so that they could stand in for them. My guess is that Roger Galloway was part of the conspiracy, but I'm not sure at this point."

"He was," admitted Joel.

"How did you know about Roberto and Duggo?" asked Jonathan.

"You'll remember that when Archibald Roring arrived at the gates," said Father, "he found the chain wrapped around the poles but the padlock open. The guards wouldn't have made such a careless oversight, not unless they were helping you fellows."

"We never anticipated an intruder," said Edward.

"Burglars seldom do," said Father. "Be that as it may, while the rest of you climbed aboard Arthur's station wagon and headed for Saint Philomena's to begin your ruse, Pierre drove Edward's van to the airport to arrange for the transport of the crated coffin to Rome. Meanwhile, Roberto and Duggo withdrew to the guardhouse, and Roger Galloway, resuming his regular duties, went about his rounds, reporting as he went on a walkie-talkie. What transpired in the mausoleum was recorded. I have a copy right here."

Father fished around inside his cassock and produced the small rectangular object which had been provided by Lieutenant Taper as we left police headquarters.

"Listen carefully," said Father, gently setting down the small cassette recorder on Saint Valeria's knee.

"*Wait a minute,*" crackled the voice of Roger Galloway as the Tumblars drew closer around the wheelchair. "*Something flashed in my beam. I'm going in there to look around.*"

"That's the guard," explained Father, "going into the crypt."

"*Come again?*" barked Duggo's voice. "*What did you say?*"

"*Something ... shiny,*" whispered Galloway.

"Pierre's ring," said Father. "Galloway didn't know that Pierre had left his ring atop the facing stone."

"*Aura-or,*" mumbled Galloway after some cloth-against-microphone sounds. Or perhaps it was closer to "*Ra-ra-ror.*"

"'On the floor,'" translated Father. "He caught sight of Pierre's monocle lens on the floor."

"*I did not catch that,*" said Duggo. "*Roger? What is happening?*"

"*Hang on,*" said Galloway.

Then came the soft bump, followed by a rolling sound, then another bump. "*Damn!*" cursed Galloway. "*I'll get it.*"

"Here the guard, who was groping his way closer to the empty niche dropped his flashlight," said Father, "You can hear it rolling to a stop against the wall, right under the facing stone."

"*Almost got it,*" grunted Galloway.

The tape was quiet for a moment, then, *"Ohhh,"* moaned Galloway softly, but then his groan was cut off by a hollow thud, followed a second later by a resounding *CLUNK!* The Tumblars all jumped at the sound. Then there was a half-second of rubbing cloth, and the settling of stone.

"Good Heavens," sighed Arthur.

"What happened?" gasped Joel.

"Roger?" squawked Duggo from the tiny speaker. *"Roger? Are you okay? Look: hold on. Roberto, he is coming! Roger? Roger—?"*

Father reached down and turned off the tape recorder.

"Well?" demanded the Tumblars severally.

"What do you think, Pierre?" asked Father. "Remember that your gold ring was found resting on the small of Galloway's back when he was found face-down on the floor. Put the sounds together in your mind, and tell me what happened."

"It sounds to me," said Pierre in a voice tense with seriousness, "that when he reached for his flashlight, Mr. Galloway bumped his head against the facing stone. I'm no stone mason. I probably didn't use enough cement. When the stone was jarred it gave way, falling forward, hitting him on the head. It was very heavy. He collapsed under the stone, which settled against his head."

"And?" asked Father in a penetrating tone.

"And," rasped Pierre, "my ring, which was resting on top of the stone, slipped off as the slab fell forward, and I guess landed on Mr. Galloway's back."

"That's what happened," said Father. "Except for one detail—"

"Oh, great," interrupted Arthur. "So now Pierre is going to be charged with negligent homicide instead of murder one."

"No," said Father, "any homicide occurring during the commission of a felony incurs the charge of murder in the first degree. It's the law."

"We're sunk," sighed Joel. "We were all in on it."

"Oh, dear," gulped Pierre. "Oh, dear."

Arthur and Edward nervously patted the shoulders of Saint Valeria, as if lending comfort in this time of sorrow. Jonathan detached himself from the rest, walked in a circle around us all, then returned to his original place, all the while rubbing his chin as if he was afraid it was going to fall off.

While the Tumblars pondered the situation, Father looked at me.

I looked at him.

He looked at me some more, and I returned the favor.

Finally, as if he'd been counting the time allotted for mental punishment in his head, he turned and spoke to the Tumblars in a gentle, lighthearted voice.

"As I said, gentlemen," he began, "any homicide occurring during the commission of a felony incurs the charge of murder in the first degree. This is causing you concern, and rightly so. I remind you, however, that for this statement to have any bearing on the situation in which you find yourselves, we must first determine that there was, indeed, a homicide and in the second place there must be evidence that a felony was in progress. Both of these assumptions I intend to refute."

"Refuting the homicide?" babbled the Tumblars, eyes wide. "How?"

"Let's listen again," said Father, pressing the rewind button for a moment, then hitting play.

"*Almost got it,*" grunted Galloway again. Silence. Then the groan, "*Ohhh,*" cut off by a thud, followed a moment by the *CLUNK!*

Father hit the stop button. "Galloway groaned in pain. His groan was cut short by a soft impact, and then we hear the stone hitting him on the head."

"Why did he moan," asked Joel, "if he wasn't hurt yet?"

"Oh, he was hurt," said Father. "But his pain came from within, not from without."

"I don't follow you," said Pierre.

"I called in a favor a short while ago," said Father, "by waking my good friend, Solomon Yung-sul Wong, from a sound sleep in order to tell me the results of the autopsy he performed on Roger Galloway. Mr. Galloway was suffering from a condition known as a *spontaneous subarachnoid hemorrhage.*"

"A spontaneous what?" gasped Joel, Edward and Jonathan, sort of like a Greek chorus. It was quite moving.

"The bursting of an aneurysm," explained Father, "a sacklike protrusion, often assumed to be congenital, on one of the arteries at the base of the brain. Blood issues forth and spreads out on the undersurface of the brain. Death can occur swiftly, or can be delayed. In some cases—like in Mr. Galloway's, according to Mr. Wong—there can be a minor such occurrence, after which the victim, thinking he's just got a dizzying headache, goes about his business. This can be followed by a more explosive rupture, which proves to be instantly fatal."

"You're saying," said Edward, "that Mr. Galloway had a minor attack earlier in the day?"

"That is actually the coroner's, not my, conclusion—but yes. There was evidence of prior bleeding, perhaps hours before, followed by a sudden massive flow—the groan we heard on the tape. That was Mr. Galloway dying. He fell forward, bumping his head against the facing stone. The slab came loose and toppled, landing on the back of his down-turned head and crushing him to the floor. It lay there until the police arrived, resting against his head."

"And Pierre's ring," said Jonathan, "simply landed in the small of the guard's back."

"Right," said Father. "And that means that you, Pierre, are no longer on the hook for murder. The timing was close—so close I hope you lose sleep just thinking about it—but Roger Galloway definitely died of natural causes."

"Is there any possibility," asked Edward, "that some eager district attorney might try to say that the falling stone caused the guard's aneurysm to burst—that Pierre is still responsible?"

"Such a rash DA would have to controvert his own coroner's testimony to do that," said Father. "Not likely to happen, not in this town."

"So where does that leave us?" asked Joel.

"I'm glad you asked," said Father. "Pierre will not be charged with homicide. Now he's only guilty—along with the rest of you—of stealing the priceless, and I must say breathtaking, Relic of Saint Valeria."

"But you said you were going to refute that, Father," said Edward.

"I said that I intended to refute the *assumption*," said Father. His eyes fell upon the woman slumped in the wheelchair who, to any disinterested passerby, appeared to have fallen asleep during his speech. "The theft of a priceless relic such as the body of Saint Valeria may well be a felony, gentlemen, though this scene in which we find ourselves—a group of strong men with a helpless woman under their power—might almost be classified as a kidnapping."

"This isn't funny, Father," said Joel.

"Indeed," said Father, turning toward him. "I find certain aspects of this situation *most* amusing. In fact, the trail of your shenanigans, once you had our beloved Saint in your possession, is hilarious. And to think that it never occurred to me."

"Pray tell, Father," said Pierre.

"What you found in volume fifteen of my *Catholic Encyclopedia*: the claim that Saint Valeria's body was discovered incorrupt when they opened her tomb in Rome to transport her to Los Angeles—just as she had been found on five separate occasions since her original interment in the fourth century. Talk about assumptions! More like a leap of Faith, I'd say. You set up this whole caper on the certainty that when you opened her casket you would find her body intact—indeed, you even trusted in the resemblance between the photograph reproduced in the encyclopedia and Arthur's sister, Beth, enough to pay for her airfare to come out here to take part in your scheme."

38

THEIR REACTION WAS DROWNED OUT by an announcement from the speaker overhead: *"TWA flight 1326 bound for Rome, Italy, will begin boarding in approximately fifteen minutes. We will be bringing you aboard in sections, so please have your boarding passes ready."*

"Ah," said Father, "speaking of Arthur's sister ..."

Monsignor Havermeyer came race-walking toward us, arm-in-arm with the delightful young woman who, the previous evening, had giggled at our applause, and then almost nodded off into her tapioca.

"I'm sorry, Arthur," said Beth as she and the monsignor joined us around the wheelchair. "Monsignor Havermeyer here came and found me at your apartment. This man is such a dear. He can bully, but he can't lie. He wanted me to come with him. First he tried to convince me that you'd been in an accident, then he said you'd been arrested in some sort of drug deal. When he finally showed me the paper with Father Baptist's instructions, and I saw that he was to bring me here to the airport, I figured the jig was up—that Father Baptist was on to you guys—so I came along for damage control."

"I'm sorry we're late, Father," puffed Monsignor Haver-meyer. "I guess I wasn't very convincing, but ... but ..." His eyes came to rest on the serene form in the wheelchair. He looked up at Beth, then down at the woman, then up and down again just to be sure. "Good Heavens, Father Baptist, who is this? The resemblance to Miss von Derschmidt is ... un-canny."

"That's what the Tumblars counted on," said Father Bap-tist. "That's why, having picked up Beth shortly before three at the airport and dropping her off at Arthur's apartment, they went to New Golgotha Cemetery—to retrieve her double from the unmarked tomb."

"How do you know that?" asked Arthur. "About the time of her flight, I mean?"

"I phoned your mother, Arthur, and asked her for the flight number. You'd better call her at the first opportunity because I promised her that you would explain everything."

"Great," sighed Arthur.

"So," continued Father, obviously enjoying himself, "having dropped off Beth at Arthur's apartment, they headed for the cemetery where they had made prior arrangements, replacing two of the night guards with Roberto and Duggo. These stand-ins stood by as the Tumblars liberated Saint Vale-ria from her unmarked niche, opened her coffin, placed her surprisingly supple body in the back seat of Arthur's station wagon, crated and loaded the casket in Edward's van, and ex-ited the cemetery. That's when the hilarity I mentioned commenced. Their actions were daring, their timing incisive, and their plan insightfully clever."

Monsignor Havermeyer's eyes went wide as the enormity of Father Baptist's words penetrated his scar-studded noggin. "Are you telling me—?"

"Exactly," said Father. "Saturday evening, when the Tumblars came by and asked us to come out to the car to meet Arthur's sister, it was this woman in the wheelchair who was propped in the back seat. They were making their geta-way from the cemetery, and they seized the opportunity to concoct an alibi. Surely they knew we'd remember them! They also knew that if the theft of Saint Valeria were ever dis-covered, I among others would turn a suspicious eye upon them. Their story about just coming from the airport gave them an implied alibi of at least an hour's activities before they dropped in on us."

"This is unnerving," said Jonathan.

"Yeah," said Arthur. "Having your own thought processes decanted for you by Father Baptist."

"As it turned out," Father said with a wink, "the theft of Saint Valeria was discovered almost immediately."

"But this," said Havermeyer, still captivated by the tranquil face of the woman in the wheelchair. "This is ... sacrilege."

"And it gets better," said Father, now almost jovial in his reconstruction of events. "Sunday morning the Tumblars brought a woman in a wheelchair to Mass where we could all get a good look at her. Like gracious gentlemen, they gently lifted her limp form into the front pew. Our hearts were going out to the real Beth, who pretended to have narcoleptic fits throughout Mass. I'll leave it to you, Beth, to figure out whether or not you met your Sunday obligation under those circumstances."

"You're wrong there, Father," said Beth, wagging her finger. "I do, too, have narcolepsy, but nothing like the persona Arthur and his friends have built around me. I nod off at any and every odd moment, but only if I don't take my medication—like I didn't Sunday morning, and that was an accident, not part of the plot. The trip had so exhausted me that I'd only managed to unpack one of my three suitcases my first night out here, and naturally my pills were in the last bag, which I didn't get to until Sunday afternoon."

"Fortuitous or not," said Father, "everyone in the parish got a good look at the woman sleeping through Mass in the front pew. There could be no doubt in anyone's mind that Arthur von Derschmidt's sister was lovely but cursed, her face beautiful but her life undermined by this cruel and intrusive disorder."

"Thanks for the almost-compliment," she countered. "'Lovely but cursed.' You make it sound far worse than it is. Sure, I can never drive a car, and some people get impatient because they think I find them boring. Well, Saint Elizabeth of Hungary, my namesake, never drove a car, and her life wasn't wasted. And I'll tell you something: most people *are* bores—don't let our little secret out!"

"The truth will out, Monsignor," said the gardener. "She did find your sermon boring."

"As for half-compliments," said Father, "I've none to give. Beth, you are beautiful, and from all ages God knew—indeed, He saw to it—that you and Saint Valeria would share similar features, even though you lived seventeen centuries apart. What I meant to say was: your loveliness, as well as your apparent plight, made a lasting impression on my parishioners—and myself. The memory of the sight of you in church carried me, at least—I'll let Martin and the monsignor speak for themselves—it carried me through Sunday evening, when they propped Saint Valeria into the back of the station wagon for another flyby at the rectory. Even Sybil Wexler and her partner, Tragg Holcomb, were fooled."

"That's the night Edward left the books," I noted.

"Thus providing the key that has brought us all together now," said Father.

"Edward gave us away?" asked Joel.

"In a sense," said Father, "but let me finish this other first. The story gets really daring when we arrive at Monday night, where we were treated to both 'Beths' in one evening—the real Beth that came out and joined us, whose laughter endeared her to us all, but who nodded off during dinner."

"That time," said Beth, "I didn't take my medication on purpose."

"This Beth," said Father, touching his hand to her shoulder, "left the party, to be replaced by glimpses of the 'sleeping Beth' through the open door to the bedroom."

"That explains something else, Father," I said. "When you and I were out on the balcony, I saw Beth sitting at the window, seemingly asleep. Then, a few minutes later, I saw her lying down when Arthur opened the bedroom door."

"That was me at the window," said Beth. "There was only the one bed in that part of Arthur's apartment, and much as I appreciate Saint Valeria here, I wasn't about to crawl onto the bed and sleep beside her. There was the chair in the adjacent sitting room, and that's where I fell asleep."

"Which is why Arthur couldn't permit Millie to stay behind and help with the cleanup," said Father to Arthur. "The risk was too great that our housekeeper would find your house-sleeper. That's another explanation I suggest you make, Arthur, and soon. Millie was offended."

"Double great," winced Arthur.

"So as I said," continued Father, "it was quite a hilarious romp—one minute it's Beth, the next it's Saint Valeria—and the rest of us unaware that you were carting around the stolen body of a great and holy Saint."

"I repeat," said Havermeyer, eyes still riveted on the woman in the wheelchair, "this is a sacrilege."

"Is it?" said Father. "That would be a matter of intention and degree."

"You said Edward gave us away," said Jonathan, looking at his companion accusingly.

"Now wait a minute," countered Edward.

"Yes, Father," urged Joel. "Tell us how."

"Simply by returning three books," said Father, "which sat on my desk unnoticed for more than twenty-four hours. When the light bulb went on it was so obvious, I suspected that Edward wanted me to figure it out." He turned to Mr. E. S. Wyndham. "Did you, Edward?"

"Well," gulped Edward. "The thought did cross my mind that we were getting in over our heads. I don't think I consciously assumed for a minute that you'd—you know—figure it all out, not just from those three books."

"Nonetheless," said Father, "and whatever your motives, Edward, those books provided the key that unlocked the secret behind your activities."

"I repeat," said Joel. "How?"

"It was easy to reconstruct your reasoning," explained Father. "From *The Incorruptibles,* which deals with the fact that some Saint's bodies have not undergone corruption in death; to *Martyrs of the Catholic Faith,* which glossed over Saint Valeria, but directed your attention to the *Catholic Encyclopedia,* which not only contained a detailed biographical sketch, but provided you with a photograph of her incorrupt body. Once it dawned on me that Saint Valeria was one so favored by Heaven, the whole tangled mystery unwound instantly."

"Thanks, Edward," said Joel sarcastically.

"You *should* be thanking him," said Father. "If he had not tipped me off, whether intentionally or not, Pierre would still be in jail, and you'd all be in water much hotter than it is at present."

"You're welcome," snapped Edward at Joel.

"Now," said Father, "we come to the assumption that a felony has been committed. When I slapped a writ of *habeas corpus* on Lieutenant Taper's desk, he had to either charge Pierre or release him. Taper knew he couldn't prove murder, not with that coroner's report in his hand. No doubt Holcomb and Wexler—well, Holcomb anyway—would have liked to charge him with burglary and grave robbing, but they couldn't prove the nature of the theft absolutely until they—or Mr. Roundhead's agents—caught up with the crate in Italy. There they ran into a snag. They'll never get near that crate."

"Why not?" asked Havermeyer.

"Because," said Father, "it was claimed at the airport in Rome by one Raphael Zaiden, who I'll wager is at this very moment restoring the casket to the very crypt from which it was taken in 1874 by order of His Holiness, Pope Pius IX. I doubt he'll ever admit to receiving stolen property, not when he and his parishioners still consider Saint Valeria to be rightfully theirs."

"What would this Zaiden want with an empty casket?" asked Havermeyer.

"That casket will only remain empty," said Father, "until Arthur von Derschmidt, Knight of the Tumblar, arrives in Rome later today accompanied by his 'sister,' whom he's taking to 'Doctor' Zaiden's 'clinic' for treatment. By this evening, Saint Valeria will be back in her proper resting place, safe from the likes of prelates like Cardinal Fulbright."

"Like I said," giggled Beth. "The jig's up."

"But why send the casket and body separately at all?" asked Havermeyer.

"It's what's known in my former occupation as a 'red herring,'" said Father. "By shipping something as memorable and obvious as an empty coffin—specifically on a flight that would make several stops on its way to Rome rather than a non-stop—Pierre drew attention away from the real point of the caper: Saint Valeria herself. It was a good idea, actually, but the unfortunate death of Mr. Galloway drew premature attention to Pierre himself as a murder suspect."

"That," admitted Pierre, "is something we didn't anticipate."

"Burglars don't expect interruptions," said Father, "and murderers don't expect witnesses. The police, on the other hand, have seen everything and therefore expect anything. That's why they're effective at what they do—most of the time."

"You took quite a risk, Pierre," said Havermeyer.

"No more than the others, really," answered Mr. Bontemps.

"And what about this Dr. Zaiden?" asked Havermeyer, turning to Father Baptist. "Where did he come from? You say he's not really a doctor. Then what is he? Why is he so interested in Saint Valeria?"

"Yes," said Father Baptist, looking the Tumblars up and down and side to side, "what about Zaiden?"

"As usual," said Arthur, "I think you're about to tell us."

"Raphael Zaiden," said Father, "is a bishop in the Maronite Rite—the same Rite as our good friend, Father Stephen Nicanor. The Maronites have long held a strong devotion to Saint Valeria, and though they didn't actually build her cathedral in Rome, they assumed control and maintenance just around the turn of the last century."

"So *Bishop* Zaiden," said Havermeyer, "resides at the cathedral from which Saint Valeria was ordered removed by Pope Pius IX. Of course he'd want to see her returned."

"Of course," said Father, "the fact that Raphael Zaiden happens to be Father Nicanor's uncle leads me to conclude that my friend and confessor was also in on this scheme. It was Fr. Nicanor that put you in contact with Bishop Zaiden, who was only too happy to receive Saint Valeria into his keeping."

"That's about it," admitted Arthur. "But how did you know I'd be taking Saint Valeria on this particular flight?"

"Sybil Wexler is an adept at the computer," said Father. "As a favor to me, she scanned the lists of airline reservations, searching for the name 'von Derschmidt.' She found a pair of reservations for Arthur and Elizabeth in first class, bound for Rome—"

39

HIS VOICE WAS DROWNED OUT by another announcement from the speaker overhead. *"TWA flight 1326 bound for Rome, Italy, will begin boarding in approximately five minutes. Please have your boarding passes ready to hand to the flight attendant."*

"Officer Wexler," Father was saying, "also found a reservation for one Beth von Derschmidt," said Father, "on flight 827, departing for Cleveland at 5:26 this afternoon. I imagine one of you fellows was going to see that she arrived at the airport on time."

"Will Bishop Zaiden's denial," asked Edward, "really be enough to squelch the felony charge against us, Father?"

"At the receiving end, at least," said Father. "The police still have enough circumstantial evidence to prove the theft at this end—and if they break Roberto and Duggo, they'll have eye witnesses to the crime as well as accessories."

"Then we're still sunk," groaned Jonathan, rubbing his chin again.

"That depends," said Father, "on the disposition of Morley Psalmellus Cardinal Fulbright, Archbishop of Los Angeles. Since the casket placed in the crypt at New Golgotha was sealed, and as archbishop the ownership of the relics falls directly to him, only he can claim the contents. In this regard I have but one trump to play. If I fail, you're all still in trouble. If I succeed, not only will you not have to face felony charges, but the crime itself will simply never have happened."

"Can a cardinal do that?" asked Beth.

"In this case," said Father, "yes."

"I don't follow you," said Havermeyer.

"Few do," said the gardener.

"As for the charge of sacrilege," said Father, lowering his tone but maintaining that delighted twinkle in his eyes, "it boils down, I think, to a matter of the lesser of two evils."

"I have something to say about that," said Pierre, getting up from the plastic molded chair. "Father Baptist, Monsignor Havermeyer: with God as my witness, I felt—we all did—that as duly-sworn Knights of the Tumblar, we had a duty to prevent, rather than commit, sacrilege."

"Here! Here!" exclaimed the others. "You tell 'em, Pierre."

"Pope Pius IX, of honored memory," said Pierre in lofty tones, "ordered that Saint Valeria be, and I quote, 'properly protected and adored by the pious people of the City of Angels.' Clearly Cardinal Fulbright—and by extension, the people of this city who lifted no cry of protest at the removal of Saint Valeria from her proper place beneath the high altar of the cathedral which bears her name—clearly the mandate of the Vicar of Christ was being ignored, if not defied outright. The Angelenos, to whom the body of Saint Valeria had been entrusted in good faith, were proving themselves unworthy of their charge."

Several of the Tumblars gripped each other's arms as Pierre continued: "So, just as the Crusaders once liberated relics from the Holy Land lest they be desecrated by the Moslems; and just as the faithful secreted treasures like *Le San Pres'que Grall* within the walls of Notre Dame Cathedral during the French Revolution; we felt it our duty to do the same in our day. We could not, in good conscience, stand idly by while Saint Valeria was consigned to obscurity by our cardinal. We took action—the only action open to us."

Father riveted Pierre with his eyes. "You said that I would not agree, but that I would understand. I hope in the future you will learn to trust me. A lot of this could have been avoided if you had come to me in the first place."

"I'm sorry to disagree," said Pierre. "But you never would have condoned our plan."

"Not the plan, perhaps," said Father. "But your intention, with that I'm in complete agreement. I've no idea—and we'll never know—what I would have advised if you had brought your concerns to my attention. We'll have to pass on that. But you just said something interesting."

"Oh?" asked Pierre. "What's that?"

"You mentioned *Le San Pres'que Grall.* I hadn't realized that you were familiar with that particular artifact and its history."

"Did I?" said Pierre, rolling his eyes as if trying to remember.

"Which suggests the answer to another puzzle," said Father. "When you were first in the interrogation room at police headquarters, I remarked that you couldn't just send an obviously ancient and valuable coffin through customs, even without a body inside, not without all kinds of certificates and authorizations. You certainly don't have that kind of influence, but yet you managed to ship the casket without any interference from the customs officers. Now how did you manage that?"

"I have the feeling," gulped Pierre, "that you're going to tell me."

"I can make an educated guess," said Father. "You mentioned the *Le San Pres'que Grall* just now. I know of only one man who has taken a particular interest in that obscure artifact. He's a man who happens to hold views similar in some respects to yours. Could it be that you recently bumped into one Roderick Roundhead at one of those social functions you gents are always crashing?"

"I give up," sighed Joel.

"Me, too," said Jonathan, exasperated.

"I made the mistake yesterday," said Father, "of assuming, when Martin and I tracked down Mr. Roundhead in connection with the theft of the same *Le San Pres'que Grall,* that he was a man consumed with the idea of the possession, rather than the preservation, of Catholic artifacts. He convinced me otherwise, though I can't condone his methods. In any case, it seems obvious to me that you and he struck up something of a rapport—a shared mission, if you will—and he agreed to help you get Saint Valeria to a place of safety. Arthur could hardly afford a first-class ticket, let alone a pair of them, to Rome. Mr. Roundhead, I assume, paid for that. He also exerted his influence, which I know to be considerable, in obtaining the necessary authorization for the transport of the casket to Rome."

"Wait a minute," said the gardener, "wasn't it Roundhead's agents that were giving the police reports of the progress of the crate?"

"Apparently," said Father, "though it does seem odd, in retrospect, that Mr. Roundhead's operatives, used as they are to the demands of their employer, never managed to catch up with that crate—even though the shipping receipt clearly indicated that the destination was Rome."

"You think they were dragging their feet?" asked the gardener.

"As per his instructions, yes," said Father.

"But his agents were providing evidence against Pierre to the police," said Havermeyer.

"To cover his own tracks," said Father, "but I don't seriously think that Roderick Roundhead would have left Pierre's neck in a noose if it came to that. Right, Pierre?"

"That was our understanding," said Pierre. "When I met Rod—Mr. Roundhead—at a smoker in the bar of the Ritz Carlton last week, my first impression was that he had Tumblar potential. News of the cardinal's decision to remove Saint Valeria from the cathedral was just trickling down through the Catholic grapevine. We had a lot to drink, he and I, and by the end of the evening we had the beginning of an understanding. After Edward told us what he'd found in the *Catholic Encyclopedia,* I approached Mr. Roundhead for assistance, and the rest is history."

"We are happy to announce," blared the speaker overhead, *"that we are about to begin boarding TWA flight 1326, departing on time for Rome. Before our regular passengers commence embarking, we are asking that anyone with special needs, such as those confined to wheelchairs, report to the flight attendants at this time."*

"That's us," said Arthur, gripping the handles of his sleeping "sister's" wheelchair. "I assume, Father, that you're not going to stop us."

"Me?" said Father. "Heavens, no. I'll remind you that you're violating a police order, but hopefully that will be a moot issue by the time you return. I'll expect a complete report at that juncture."

"Thank-you, Father," smiled Arthur, nudging the wheelchair into motion. "We won't forget this."

"Thank-you, thank-you, Father," said the Tumblars, moving along beside Arthur.

"Go on, go on," said Father, motioning them by with a wave of his arm. "Say your farewells."

Father Baptist, Monsignor Havermeyer, and I stood there watching as the Tumblars and Beth escorted Arthur and his charge to the boarding gate.

"They're crazy, Father," said Havermeyer. "You realize that."

"What does that say about me?" said Father.

"As I've said before," huffed the monsignor, "you're either a Saint or a son-of-a-bitch, and I certainly can't tell which."

"But consider, Mon Señor," said the gardener, "what that says about you."

"Don't I know," said Havermeyer, breaking into a grin. "And you know what, Father, Martin? I wouldn't trade my association with you two for all the gold in all the collection plates in the world."

"I'll take that as a compliment," said Father.

"I guess that makes us all nuts," said the gardener.

"Speaking of which," said Father, "what time is it, Martin?"

"Quarter to five," I answered. "Time for bed."

"Hardly," said Father. "Now you and I are going to pay a visit to Cardinal Fulbright."

"At this hour?" squeaked Monsignor Havermeyer and myself in unison, hardly Greek chorus material.

"I can't think of a better time," said Father, "to play my bluff. I may be exhausted, but the cardinal will be sleepy and not yet running on all cylinders. I'm counting on that slim advantage. Come, Martin. Monsignor, I don't know if we'll get home in time for morning Mass."

"You can count on me," said Havermeyer. "I'd be honored to say it."

"The parish ladies will see that you're compensated," I said as we all turned to leave.

"Great," said Havermeyer, rubbing his tummy.

"My sister is suffering from narcolepsy," we heard Arthur telling a sympathetic flight attendant as we headed for the exit.

"It's a sleeping disorder, nothing contagious. I'll be with her the whole time. All she needs is to be left alone ..."

40

"I STILL DON'T SEE," grumbled Cardinal Fulbright, "why this couldn't wait until a reasonable hour."

He was standing there in his bathrobe and slippers, rubbing his bump with one hand, and clutching the edge of his mahogany trophy case with the other.

"It's as I told you, Your Eminence," said Father Baptist, standing his ground with the nylon bag behind his back, "Mr. Feeney and I have just come back from a harrowing journey through the dark underworld of this city. More on that, perhaps, later. I have good news for you, but there's a price."

"I already gave you a substantial sum of cash," snarled Fulbright. "Wasn't that enough?"

"Almost," said Father. "But the situation was more complicated than I anticipated. The return of your cherished chalice, the gift from Professor Murkenstein, has become contingent on the disposal of the matter of Saint Valeria."

"Who?" coughed the cardinal, shifting his rubbing from his bump to his bleary left eye. "Oh, her. I don't see the connection."

"In a day or two," said Father, "I expect a startling bit of news to come through ecclesiastical channels: the chance discovery of the tomb of Saint Valeria in the crypt beneath her cathedral in Rome."

"Bosh," scoffed he cardinal. "Her body has been here in Los Angeles for over a century."

"I wonder how many people are aware of that fact," said Father Baptist.

"Well," said the cardinal, "it's a matter of record. It's even in our tour brochures."

"Yes," said Father, "but the fact is that Saint Valeria's casket has remained sealed since long before you were raised to the episcopate. You've never ordered that her coffin be opened, have you?"

"Of course not. Why should I?"

"No reason, no reason. I'm simply pointing out that you have no certain knowledge of what was actually in that coffin when you ordered its transfer to New Golgotha Cemetery. That coffin was stolen Saturday evening, and the police are doing their best to ascertain who may have done the deed."

"So?"

"So the whole issue becomes moot the moment Bishop Raphael Zaiden announces the discovery of Saint Valeria's body under his very cathedral."

"But that's outrageous," snarled the cardinal. "She's rightfully mine."

"Of course," said Father, "you could make a formal public protest, but that would result in an investigation not just by the police, but by certain authorities in the Vatican. Are you sure you want that to happen? Your records scrutinized, your collection of relics and artifacts inventoried by clerks from the Holy See? It's likely that the sale of artifacts—transactions authorized by Your Eminence—will come to light. You had your reasons—and as your humble servant, I accept your decisions without comment—but you may well find yourself in the embarrassing position of having to explain—"

"I see your point," said Fulbright, eyes flaming and bump glowing. "So what do you suggest?"

"Silence," said Father Baptist. "Silence is your best weapon in this instance. When Bishop Zaiden makes his announcement, I suggest you say nothing. When the police make their inquiries, you might go so far as to suggest the word 'hoax,' but on second thought, don't even say that. You yourself have no certain knowledge that the body of Saint Valeria was ever here at all, and you're not even going to notify your insurance carrier of the theft. Even the best of attorneys couldn't shake more from you on the witness stand—"

"Do you think it will come to that?" gasped the cardinal. "Me, the cardinal archbishop, forced to testify in open court?"

"Not if you resort to silence now," said Father, "before the flames of suspicion get fanned into a blaze of ruthless litigation."

"But just how," growled the cardinal, "did Saint Valeria wind up back in Rome?"

"I think it best that you never know," said Father.

"What?!?!"

"What you don't know, you can't be forced to reveal," said Father. "Not by the police, not by a clever attorney, and not by a judge out to make a name for himself."

"I think you have something there," said Fulbright, rubbing his bump again like a security blanket. "It seems odd coming from you, Father Baptist, but then you never cease to surprise me."

"Speaking of surprises," said Father, bringing the nylon bag out from behind his back, "I have something here for you."

"What is it?"

"See for yourself," said Father, handing it to him.

With suspicious fingers, the cardinal unzipped the bag. His face went through a number of contortions—most of them related to "elation," I think, but with his face it was hard to tell—as he pulled out the glistening cup and held it up to the light.

"Oh!" he gasped—indeed, he almost drooled. "Oh, Father Baptist, you found it!" He began to turn it every which way, admiring every millimeter of its unabashed ugliness. Suddenly, his smile fell. "Wait a minute. What's this on the inside?" He sniffed the cup. "Ashes? Someone was using my chalice for ... an *ashtray?*"

"That's the kind of travesty," said Father, "that comes when sacred objects fall into unbelieving hands, Your Eminence."

"The man who stole it did this?"

"No," said Father. "It passed through several hands before I discovered its whereabouts. Who's to say who abused it along the way?"

"But I told you I wanted the thief brought to justice."

"I doubt the culprit will ever be apprehended. His tracks are cold, and besides, he's just a go-between."

"And what about the man you gave my money to?"

"He keeps himself well-hidden," said Father. "Martin and I were taken to him in a car with blackened windows. We never saw where we were going."

"You're serious," said the cardinal, cradling his precious, though admittedly stinking, cup. "When you mentioned the underworld, you weren't kidding."

"I'm just grateful that the man was willing to sell," said Father. "Your Eminence, do consider the matter settled. You have your chalice back, and now you have a better appreciation for what can happen to sacred vessels when they pass from under your august protection."

"Indeed I do," said the cardinal, squinting at the black residue in his precious cup.

"By your leave," said Father.

"What?" blinked the cardinal. "Oh yes, of course."

"May we have your blessing?" asked the gardener.

"Huh?" blinked the cardinal a second time. "Oh, very well." He waved a vague Sign of the Cross in our direction as we made our departure.

"You chose your words carefully," I whispered to Father Baptist as we descended a flight of marble stairs to the street below.

"Always," winked Father. "Words, as you know, mean exactly what they say."

41

DAWN WAS STREAMING IN through the window as Father Baptist and his loyal gardener stood beside the hospital bed in room 304.

"I see that you've returned to us," smiled Father, resting his hip on the edge of Willie Kapp's mattress.

"Ah, Jack," groaned the face on the pillow, "you no idea where Willie has been. Oh, dah skull it hurt, mon. Tell dah guys wit dah jackhammers dey can go home."

"I can call a nurse," suggested the gardener.

"Naw," groaned Willie. "Dey ain't got wot Ah need."

"And what do you need?" asked Father.

"Willie gave you trust," said Willie.

"And I have it right here," said Father, producing the stained leather pouch about the size of a tuna sandwich, still tied at the throat with a soiled yellow cord.

"Ah knew you good, Jack," said Willie, accepting the pouch with trembling fingers. "Willie knew you Ah could trust."

"Do you want to tell me about it?" asked Father. "The man who broke into your shop and knocked you out—was this what he wanted?"

"Hah hah," laughed Willie. His chortle turned into a gasp, then a fit of coughs, then finally settled down into a seesawing wheeze.

"Take your time," said Father quietly.

"Dah mon who broke into mah shop," said Willie at last, "he hit Willie, but he take dah wrong pouch."

"How do you know?"

"Silly mon, Ah know because dere was only one pouch in dah store—dah fake I Ah left in plain sight. Dah real one—dis one here—dat was wit' you. Ah know he was comin', and Ah know he'd turn mah place inside out to find it when he come, so Ah left dah fake right on dah countertop. Ah didn't 'spect him to hit Willie, but dat's dat."

"Hm," said Father. "That pouch must contain something very important indeed."

"Jack, mah fren, wit' all dat you know and believe, you have no idea."

"Well," said Father, slipping off the edge of the bed, "now you have it back, and Martin and I will be going."

"Don't forget to take dah jackhammers wit' you," rasped Willie, slipping the pouch under the covers and clutching it to himself like a teddy bear.

"Oh, one thing," said Father, "before we go."

"Sure, mon."

"It's about favors."

"Sure, Jack. Watchoo wan', mon?"

"Not me," smiled Father. "You. You asked favors."

"Did Ah?"

"First, you asked me to come, and I came."

"Dat's right, Jack. You come, fo' sure."

"Second, you asked me to take the pouch for safe keeping—not to open it, and not to tell anyone about it."

"Dat's so. Willie ask for trust, an' Father Jack give trust."

"Then you called again—Martin answered the phone, remember?—and asked me to come yet again."

"Dat's number t'ree. See? Even wit' broken skull, Willie's brain still work—sort of."

"As I understand it," said Father, "three favors—"

"Is dah most, Jack, dah most dah hon'rable mon can ask dah fren in one day."

"But when Martin and I arrived at your shop and found that you'd been hurt, you were about to ask a fourth favor."

"Ah 'member it well, mon. Ten minutes 'til midnight. So sue me."

"Well," said Father, "you passed out. That was Saturday night, now it's Tuesday morning."

"So?"

"So you can ask me that last favor now without dishonor. What was the fourth favor you wanted?"

"Ah," said Willie, licking his lips with a dry, caked tongue. "To ask, Jack, to ask you never to ask me to tell you wot's in dis pouch."

"Never?" asked Father.

"No, never," said Willie. He turned his coconut eyes on me. "You, too, Martin Mon."

"What?" I yelped, thinking of the risk Father had taken in hiding that infernal pouch behind a loose stone in the church, what with Tragg hanging around making all those innuendoes—and not to mention my own unsatisfied curiosity! "Of all the—"

I was cut short by the look in Father Baptist's eyes, a penetrating glare that seemed to whisper, commanding yet humbly, "Considering all the secrets we've added to our larder in the past three days, Martin, is one thing more really going to matter?" But all he actually said—to me more than to Willie—was, "Agreed."

"T'anks, Jack," sighed Willie, his eyelids starting to droop.

"You owe me one, though."

"No, Ah owe you t'ree."

"I can't argue with that," smiled Father.

"Please don't," mumbled Willie, sinking into sleep. "Jackhammers."

"What's that, Willie?" asked Father, leaning close.

"Don't forget ... to take ... dah jackhammers ... wit' you..."

Wednesday, November Fifteenth

**Feast Day of Saint Albertus Magnus,
scientist and theologian, some say magician,
teacher of Saint Thomas Aquinas,
Doctor of the Church (1280 AD)**

∞ Epilogue ∞

42

"WELL, MARTIN," SAID FATHER BAPTIST, sitting across from me in the garden. "What do you think of our lawyer?"

"I dunno," I shrugged, thinking that this was the last question in the world I expected to answer at that moment. "Mr. de Montfort is okay, I guess. It's not like I'd invite him to go bowling or something—"

"Not our attorney," laughed Father. "The lawyer arguing with Christ in Saint Luke's Gospel."

"Who?" I asked, waiting for my brain to engage. "Oh, of course, the discussion we were having a few days ago when Sybil Wexler erupted ... I mean, interrupted."

"Words mean what they say, Martin."

"At least they once did, Father."

"Yes, Martin. They did once."

It was evening, around nine o'clock. This being Los Angeles, there were few stars bright enough to penetrate the umbrella of airborne debris of which we Angelenos are so proud. Still, Saturn was having the last word with Jupiter, and the Big Dipper was dry and wondering why as usual.

"So the lawyer," said Father, whose outline I could barely make out in the darkness.

"Oh, him," I said. "Well, he was just trying to put himself in the best possible light, you know. I'm not defending him, you understand, but we all do that."

"You mean we argue with God?"

"Well, I certainly do."

Father Baptist's dark silhouette seemed to fold its arms. "The trouble with that approach, however, is that in flaunting our pale brilliance against the Light of Light, we only show our shallow contempt for His Omnipotence. Where does that leave us?"

"Right about where we are, Father."

Father sighed. "So why do we keep doing it?"

"Because we like where we are—or at least we try to convince ourselves that we do. I never said we make sense. Our nature is, after all, fallen."

I was propped against the cement birdbath and he was seated on the bench. The traffic beyond the gates hummed and thrummed, routing human cells through every vein and artery of the metropolitan circulatory system. The City of Angels had lost her heart when the Tumblars put Saint Valeria on that jet bound for Europe—perhaps her soul, too, as well as her strength and mind. Yet somehow the cells still flowed, the collective stomach still consumed, the superconscious liver went on processing poisons, and somewhere out there Pierre and the Knights Tumblar were having a sleepless night. The world was fallen, but not paralyzed.

"I've been meaning to ask you," I said presently. "Do you think that Tragg Holcomb and Sybil Wexler will press charges against Pierre or the others?"

"Unlikely," said Father. "By now our beloved cardinal has lapsed into Holy Silence—let's enjoy that blessing while we can—and I understand that the unsinkable Monsignor Aspic has made much use of the word 'hoax' to all concerned. For a theft to be declared a felony the stolen item must have considerable worth, yet the cardinal isn't even notifying the insurance company. No, Martin, it's as I said it would be: the crime never happened."

"But Father, when word gets out that Saint Valeria's presence here in Los Angeles was a hoax, won't that hurt the faithful?"

"Frankly, Martin, there are not that many faithful left. You saw how great an outcry her removal from the high altar produced. You saw how many accompanied her to the mausoleum. No, if the Chancery Office declares Saint Valeria a hoax, most Catholics around here will just nod their heads and go about their business."

"The old what-ever-Father-says syndrome," I sighed. "Only in this case, it's the cardinal himself."

"Exactly. It's wrong, it's not truly Catholic, but it's become the norm. It wasn't always that way. Centuries ago, when a bishop named Nestorious got up in the pulpit and announced that Mary was not the Mother of God, the people rose as one and cried, 'We have no bishop!' They threw him out into the street."

"Today," I mused, "they'd just put another dollar in the collection plate and go back to sleep."

"Yes, unfortunately."

"It's sad."

"But take heart, my friend," said Father Baptist. He filled his lungs with the crisp night air. "Those who are more informed, and therefore self-reliant in matters of the Faith, they will know better. My mother used to pray before the high altar at Saint Valeria's whenever she and Dad were having money worries and illnesses. When she prayed, she got results—sometimes material, sometimes not—but she always got results. My own ordination, I believe, was the result of her devotion. There's no way you or the cardinal himself could convince her that Saint Valeria was not there to answer her prayers. After all, to those who believe, no proof is necessary."

"And to those who don't believe," quoth the gardener, "n o proof is necessary, either."

"Well said."

A jet roared by overhead, its lights blinking as it banked for its approach to LAX. Father and I watched as it faded in the smog.

"Well," I said at last, rubbing my hands against the chill, "in the spirit of Willie 'Skull' Kapps, keeper of the notorious skellkurg and a medal of Our Lady of Guadalupe—"

"You're about to mention three favors," smiled Father—at least, I think he smiled. It was dark, but I was sure I saw two twinkles where his eyes should have been.

"It's what any honorable man would do," I explained.

"And we are honorable men, I hope," said Father. "But this is a poor parish. Tell you what: we'll split the three favors—you and I."

"How do you split three favors between two people, Father?"

"Well," he said sagaciously, "you take one, then I'll take one, and then we'll share the third."

"Sounds cockeyed to me, but okay. You want me to go first?"

"Of course, Martin."

"Okay, Father. For my favor I'd like to ask you what you've got hidden under your cassock tonight. I distinctly heard something clink when you sat down on that bench, and my curiosity is piqued."

"You *are* getting observant in middle age," said Father. "You didn't have to ask, really, because I had every intention of showing you."

"Leave it to me," I chuckled, "to waste my first wish."

"It's not wasted," said Father, unraveling something which he produced from the mysterious folds of his cassock. "This arrived this afternoon. It was postmarked Van Nuys."

"Cash?" I asked. "That doesn't clink."

"No, nothing as mundane as money," said Father. "Here, I'm handing you a match so you can see it clearly."

I felt the brittle wooden stick pressed against my fingers. Scraping it against the pockmarked rim of the cement bird-bath on which I was sitting—and bumping my friend, the little porous bird in the process—I held the match out in front of me. The spark in the dark hissed into a gush of orange flame. When I saw what Father was holding in his hands, I almost burned myself.

It was simple, but made of gold. It was ancient, and yet looked as though it had been fashioned only yesterday. During the two thousand years of its existence, it had been used, hoarded, liberated, sold, venerated, secreted, auctioned, donated, and stolen. Someone had once called it, "the least sacred of all." I called it the only name I could pronounce:

"The Holy next to the Grail."

"Yes, Martin," said Father, turning it reverently in his hands, *"Le San Pres'que Grall.* I can't let you touch it, you see, because it's been used to celebrate Mass."

"No problem," I gulped. "I'm perfectly willing to just be 'next to' such a beautiful relic. You must be very pleased, Father. What do you intend to do with it?"

"Well," said Father, tucking it away, "the cardinal said nothing about wanting it back. Mr. Roundhead must have his reasons for sending it here. I suppose I might just say Mass with it myself, perhaps on special occasions, such as when the Tumblars celebrate their Saints' Days. There's a little nook behind a loose stone in the church—I think this will just about fit."

"I told you Roderick Roundhead might be Tumblar material," I smiled. "I—yikes!" Just then the flame reached my thumb and forefinger. I let the match fall, the tiny blaze flickering out as it disappeared into the darkness around my feet.

"That must've hurt," observed Father.

"Mm-hmm," I mumbled, sucking my injury. "I'll live."

"My turn," said Father Baptist. "The second favor of the day is: I'd like to see what you've got concealed under your coat, my friend."

"Who, me?" I asked innocently.

"I distinctly heard something clink against that birdbath when you sat down."

"Well," I said, "you know that I took the pledge not to drink alcohol years ago, Father, long before I met you."

"Yes, Martin. I also know that every time I solve a crime, you bring another bottle of wine out from that case you have hidden in your closet. I suppose you want me to grant you a dispensation for the evening."

"That would have been my third favor," I admitted, slipping the bottle out from under my coat. "But—"

"Ah, the third favor," said Father. "The one we're going to share."

"The very one."

"Here, Martin, strike another match for me, will you?"

He pressed a match in my hand, and I struck it against the birdbath. As light reached out from the flame, I saw that Father Baptist was holding two crystal wine glasses.

He shrugged his shoulders. "I said we'd share."

I held the flame up to the label on the bottle. *Lacrimæ Christi*, it said, in long fancy letters. Dropping the match into the darkness, I uncorked the bottle and poured the obliging wine by feel into the glasses in Father's hands.

"The Tears of Christ," I toasted.

"The Tears of Christ," answered Father, touching his glass to mine. "And here's to Saint Valeria."

"To Saint Valeria," I sighed. "May she finally rest in peace."

THE END

—Init: September 13, 1998
Traditional Feast of Saint Eulogius, Confessor (608 AD),
Modern Feast of Saint John Chrysostom,
Bishop and Doctor of the Church (407 AD)

—Finis: September 23, 1998
Appropriately:
The Feast of Our Lady of Ransom

Rock Haven.

Coming soon!

Out of the Depths

*The fourth book in the continuing saga of
Fr. John Baptist, the cop-turned-priest, and
Martin Feeney, his gardener-turned-chronicler.*

From